Jingles and Me

By Margaret Eldridge

is released to celebrate Margaret's 85th Birthday.

Photo courtesy of Minh Hien and Farshid

Jingles and Me contains a collection of jingles written by Margaret Eldridge over many years to celebrate friendships and to raise funds for various causes. There are jingles to raise funds for the *Dogs' Homes of Tasmania* as dogs are an important part of Margaret's life. There are jingles to raise funds for Motor Neurone Disease research in Tasmania, a cause that is dear to Margaret's heart. There are jingles for friends and family to make them laugh as Margaret loves to see smiles on their faces. There are jingles to celebrate friendships, communities, birthdays, marriage, well-being, healthy living and farewells. By publishing these jingles, after much persuasion, Margaret shares her life with us.

For
my much loved family
and
those who have encouraged me to write jingles
and yet more jingles!

Published in 2022 by Minh Hien Pty Limited
ABN 86 086 458 817
www.minh-hien.com

Acknowledgements: We thank Janice Luckman and Ellyse Tran for allowing us to use the photos of their paintings and sketches. Our gratitude goes to Tri Tri Tran, for allowing us to take photos of Ellyse's paintings and sketches.

Inquiries should be addressed to
Minh Hien Pty Limited
PO Box 737
Drummoyne NSW 1470
Australia.

This book is released under the brand name *Wealthy Me* ® from the Hobart office of Minh Hien Pty Limited in Albion Heights Drive, Kingston, 7050. Tasmania.

Title: *Jingles and Me*
Author: Margaret Eldridge
Compilers: Hien Minh Thi Tran (Minh Hiền) and Farshid Anvari
ISBN: 978-0-9946028-8-6 (Hardback)

A catalogue record for this book is available from the National Library of Australia

A cheerful heart is good medicine,
but a crushed spirit dries up the bones.

The Bible, the Book of Proverbs 17:23

CONTENTS

Book cover photos:

Margaret Eldridge, Maning Avenue, Sandy Bay, TAS.

View from Minh Hien and Farshid's office, Albion Heights Drive, Kingston, TAS.

About the Creators of this Book

Margaret Eldridge is a mother, a grandmother, a teacher, an actor, a singer, a reader, a copy editor and the author of *New Mountain, New River, New Home? The Tasmanian Hmong*. She has taught English as a second language, and provided support and care for numerous refugees and migrants for over forty years. In 2007, she was awarded the AM for services to international students, migrants and refugees. She is a loving mother of four children and a caring grandmother of eight grandchildren and three step-grandchildren. She migrated to Tasmania in 1964 from the UK. She has numerous friends in Hobart and worldwide. She has written many jingles, some of which are here in print. She wishes to make people smile and to raise funds for various causes that are dear to her heart. This book captures some of the special times in her life and the lives of her friends. Margaret holds a Bachelor of Arts, a Graduate Diploma in Educational Studies (TESOL) and a Master of Arts, all from the University of Tasmania and an Honorary degree in Education from Roehampton University, UK. She lives in Hobart with her two faithful dogs. Feature stories and articles about her achievements have appeared in the *Mercury*, the *University of Tasmania Alumni Magazine* and on the

https://www.womenoftheisland.com/an-open-door

https://tasmaniantimes.com/2017/03/mysterious-hmong/

https://immigrationplace.com.au/story/margaret-eldridge/

https://www.abc.net.au/news/2015-09-01/hmong-community-celebrates-each-day-of-40-years-in-tasmania/6740146

Hien Minh Thi Tran (Minh Hiền) and Farshid Anvari are the designers of this book. They love to record life experiences and to capture the beauty and happiness of life through books. They have co-created *Australian Vietnamese Golf Association (AVGA): for Love of the Game; Growing Up with Papa; Wealthy Me Goldsbrough; Wealthy Me® Academy*. Minh Hiền has also authored *My Heritage: Vietnam fatherland motherland*. They have presented academic papers at international conferences and published research papers in international journals in the fields of education, engineering, computing, accounting and management since 1989. Minh Hiền and Farshid live in Sydney and Hobart.

In Due Course

It may be a day,
It may be a week,
It could be a month,
Or even a year.
Whenever it comes
Due course will surely appear!

Be patient and wait,
Through periods of time,
Through decades and eras,
Whatever their source.
There's virtue in waiting
And anticipating
The timeless expression
"In Due Course."

Dr Kathleen (Kate) McPherson (1956 – 2007)

Jingles and Me

When I heard my brother Richard and his wife Joan were coming to Tasmania from Canada for my 85th birthday, I decided I would mark the occasion with a book of my jingles. Sadly, their plans changed but I've gone ahead with the book because of the wonderful help of my friends Minh Hien and Farshid.

Minh Hien was a student of mine in the 80s and we renewed our friendship more recently when she published her book, *My Heritage: Vietnam fatherland motherland*. I have subsequently done some editing and proof reading of her writing and now she is doing the same for me. Serendipity! In addition, Farshid's computer skills are an enormous asset. But, as they say, any mistakes are my responsibility!

It seems I have been writing jingles for ages but the first ones I can find, date back to my days as an ESL teacher with the Adult Migrant English Service. I wrote for the farewell occasions of Gloria Keil and Sister Philip Cowmeadow. Gloria's was sung to Click go the Shears and all the staff joined in to send Gloria off to retirement. From then on, jingles became part of my persona. Inspired by a variety of things and sometimes at the request of others, I wrote jingle upon jingle.

This book is primarily for my family and friends but I shall also use it to raise funds for Motor Neurone Disease (MND) Research.

I helped to care for my dear friend Dr Kate McPherson who succumbed to this dreadful disease. Before she died, aged 51, I promised her I would raise funds for research into this horrific illness, as long as I was able. By persuading folk to buy a copy of *Jingles and Me*, hopefully I can have one last major fund-raising effort as it becomes more difficult for me to add to the thousands of dollars my aqua friends have helped me raise. A second friend Doreen Walker was also a victim and so was Gloria for whom the first jingle was written. Who would have guessed she would be another victim?

Minh Hien's dear mother also died of MND aged 51 so there is another reason to publish this book and fundraise for MND.

Vale Gloria

(Sing to Click Go the Shears)

Here's to the one who's about to retire
She has been AMES's home tutor live wire.
Life with ESL will never be the same,
Now we'd better tell you this terrific lady's name!
Chorus.
Gloria Gloria Gloria Gloria, Gloria, Gloria Keil
Gloria, Gloria, Gloria will leave us in a while,
Gloria, Gloria, Gloria we think you're great!
Gloria, Gloria, Gloria, our very good mate!

Migrants have reason to shed a few tears.
Gloria has been their good friend for so many years,
Training their tutors to teach them very well,
Her co-ordinating will be missed we can tell!
Chorus.

Illustrations numerous she's done for us all,
Working so cleverly beyond duty's call.
Stories have poured out and made us all smile,
Life at AMES without our union rep. will be a trial!
Chorus.

So here's to our friend who's about to retire
We hope retirement brings you your heart's desire.
Time to paint the shack and potter on the beach,
But we won't be surprised of you come back to teach!!!
Chorus.

Au Revoir Sister Phil

They said "Please bring a ditty"
As Phil heads off from the city.
In some ways it's a pity
That she's going to go.

The old team's rent asunder
As we lose our saintly wonder.
Will the heavens crash with thunder?
Now she's going to go?

Our staff is getting thinner
And St James will be the winner,
For our Phil's no rank beginner
But she's going to go.

We'll miss her sense of humour
But I've heard a little rumour
That they'll welcome and consume her
Since she's going to go.

So put your hands together
And wish her sunny weather.
Her cap has a new feather,
And she's going to go.

I'll have to end this vignette
(Well, nothing rhymes with Cygnet)
We can't hold her with a big net
Now it's time to go.

Move to 43 Maning Avenue 1998

When I moved in to 43 Maning Avenue, my next door neighbour Sue Hutchinson, organised a welcome morning tea. I sang this modification of the old shaker song to those who welcomed me and I added to it years later.

They sang of a valley of love and delight;

I feel I have come to a similar site.

I've neighbours who greet me

And come out to meet me;

This end of the road is just right!

And many years later

With happiness greater.

This home has been fine

For all of this time

And I still rank it for sure a first-rater.

At this end of my life

I avoid much strife

And I've shared my home

With many who've come

To escape the torture that's rife.

I've shared it with dogs,

Heated it with logs

Built me a garden

Please beg your pardon

But never allowed any mogs.

Asylum I 're offered them,

Peace I have shared with them,

They have recovered

And we have discovered

Some meaning for life.

43 Maning Ave before the garden was established.

Ready to move to 43 Maning Ave

Maning Avenue Christmas

Our Christmas do has come again,
This year it's changed location;
Sally and Dean have taken on
This annual occasion.

Lisa and Danny, bless them both,
Have hosted it for years,
But now we'll struggle up the hill
And reach the top in tears!

Our neighbours all assembled here
Are really a delight;
I'll do my best to recall names
But I may not get it right!

But names are not the only thing
I'll struggle with tonight;
This vast array of food and drink,
So tempting, every bite!

Our street is quite a friendly place
We meet and greet our neighbours;
And when a village meeting's called
We pause from all our labours.

We catch up on the local goss,
We listen so sincerely
In case someone needs helping out,
We like to be there, really.

People sick or babies new
Or people moving in,
We welcome them in numerous ways
And might put out their bin.

Our Bushcare group is very small,
But welcomes new assistance;
Cotoneaster, hawthorn, weeds.
We attack them with persistence!

But what a space that bushland is,
It's such a special place.
We share it with our furry friends
And birdlife of such grace.

It's quiet here in Maning Ave
Apart from dogs and motors,
The dogs of course are truly loved
By all the local voters,

We love our gardens, in this street
We even trade our seedlings,
And take a chance on what comes up
Even if it's weedlings.

I bless the day that I moved here,
This wonderful location,
With space to breathe and run about
A truly good sensation.

So Maning people one and all,
We've gathered for a reason,
Let's not forget to spread goodwill
Throughout the Christmas season!

Myrtle Cottage 2013

RIP For Des's Suzuki Swift

My good friend Des, with whom I shared several holidays, drove a yellow Suzuki Swift but eventually parted from it in favour of a four-wheel drive which he brought to Hobart on two occasions, when he drove it around the State. We also had two holidays on the mainland including one when we drove the outback to Lake Mungo. That was spectacular.

Clancy and My Surprise follow a jingle about Des' Suzuki.

Then a jingle about my latest car - a Toyota Prius hybrid.

> So where do old Suzukis go
>
> When bodies wear and gaskets blow?
>
> When on the clock the numbers climb
>
> You're forced to wonder, is it time
>
> To leave behind this earthly race
>
> So memories can take their place?
>
> It's served you well and done its best;
>
> It looks as if it's time to rest.
>
> Prepare to leave your long-time friend;
>
> The journey's up, you're at road's end.
>
> But gaskets go and gaskets come;
>
> It shouldn't cost a princely sum.
>
> Mechanics know just what to do
>
> To make Suzukis good as new!

2000

Clancy

I wonder, can you see him
As he rides behind the herd?
It's Clancy and he's riding
Even though his figure's blurred.

I wonder, can you hear him
As he droves the cattle on?
I'm sure he will be singing
For the legend lingers on.

The Clancys of the here and now
So rarely ride a horse;
They follow up the cattle
On a motorbike of course.

But still his spirit lingers,
You can see him if you will
As the drovers move the cattle
In outback regions still.

Written in the outback. 2000

My Surprise

You took me to the outback,
You opened up my eyes.
We drove the silent roadway
And you talked of a surprise.

You turned the car and parked it,
And asked me to get out.
The air was cool, yet perfumed
And I slowly looked about.

What was I meant to see here?
It really wasn't clear
Until you pointed upwards.
The stars were just so near.

This was a magic moment
As we looked up to the skies,
To stars and constellations
As promised- my surprise!

Saga of my Prius

I bumped a curb and got a flat
Which really was a worry,
A helpful soul rang RACT
And they came in a hurry.

Some time went by, another flat.
This time it was a nail.
At Bob Jane T mart, two new tyres,
Just part of the Prius tale.

More to come for my little car.
A bus hit me from the side.
Took my wing mirror in one blow
Talk about a ride!

A service at Toyota,
Repairs were needed too.
That bus had slightly clipped me
As buses shouldn't do!

I paid the bill at Toyota;
The bloke said "By the way,
You realise you have no spare."
Well, what was I to say?

Back to Bob Jane T mart;
Asked them to explain
Why my spare tyre wasn't there,
And just the two new tyres remain.

An oversight, they told me,
Apologised and all.
Gave me a brand, new spare tyre.
That was a lucky call.

The moral of this story is
Take care when you drive.
Avoid kerbs and nails and buses
And hopefully you'll survive.

January 2022

Minh Hien and Margaret with the Toyota Prius hybrid
Photo courtesy of Farshid Anvari

Dr Margaret Baikie AM etc! Sophia meeting, July 2009

In 2009 my dear friend and mentor Margaret Baikie, was awarded the AM for her varied voluntary work. We celebrated at a meeting of our Christian Women's group Sophia. Margaret and Sophia have been very important facets of my life and I acknowledge that here.

Our Margaret's got the Aussie gong

For all her volunteering.

She's now Doc Margaret AM;

(The medal's soon appearing!)

We wonder how she does it all;

The refugees etcetera.

She fits in all her family things.

It just gets better and betterer.

Her work for Lifeline and Red Cross,

That too has now been mentioned,

Along with medical deeds galore.

How long before she's pensioned?

In humbleness, with dignity

Margaret accepts her medal.

It just amazes all of us,

She refuses to back-pedal.

Congratulations Margaret dear

From Sophia (at Tarooner).

We honour you and say "Well done!"

It should have happened sooner!!!

Thorns may hurt you,
men desert you,
sunlight turn to fog;
but you're never friendless ever,
if you have a dog.

Douglas Malloch

Photo courtesy of Janice Luckman, from her painting of Jonas.

Tess 1990 - 2002

After six traumatic months renting in Taroona, my lovely dog Tess and I found our forever home as mentioned but four years later, Tess succumbed to a nasty oesophageal cancer and left a huge hole in my life. I missed her terribly. She had seen me through some dark days, made easier because of her constant companionship. My dogs have been essential to my life. I must have written jingles about other dogs but I cannot find them. Kita was probably the most special, highly intuitive and devoted companion. Then came Gabby, always good for a jingle!

The blankets are washed

And the lead hangs still.

The basket is empty,

The kennel too.

The bowl's in the cupboard

Her tag's in the drawer.

No "Welcome home."

Or wag of the tail.

No nudge to say "Mealtime."

No "Please let me out."

No guard by my bed,

No lick of the hand.

The friend who has shared

My good days and bad,

Who revelled in walks,

Was everyone's friend,

The neighbourhood's "Clayton's"

Their substitute dog

Could not beat the odds.

My precious companion

Who gave me so much,

Her love overflowing,

But now it's farewell.

Gabby

We got her from the Dogs' Home
She'd been a Gagebrook stray,
She must have had a family
Before she ran away.

We looked at her on Tuesday,
On Thursday picked her up;
She stressed out at the Dogs' Home,
But she's just a ten month pup.

The Dogs' Home called her Gabby
And I thought that was fine,
I think it really suits her
And I love her now she's mine!

She's small in size and sable,
Her markings are quite neat,
And when she puckers up a frown,
Her wrinkles are quite sweet.

I take her to the beach each day,
She freaks out at the waves,
But how she loves the other dogs
And mostly she behaves!

She's really very gentle
At least, most of the time,
But she can be quite excitable,
But, hey, that's not a crime.

Thank goodness she is house-trained,
And sits when she is told.
She's learned to jump into the car;
She's slowly growing bold.

She's been to puppy training,
I think she did quite well,
But mostly played with other dogs;
She'll train well I can tell.

There is one disadvantage,
She cries when I go out.
I'm hoping that in time she'll learn
I'll be back without a doubt.

I think my darling Kita
Would understand my choice.
I think she'd say "Good on you mum".
I can almost hear her voice.

She'd know I could not live alone,
And that I miss her so,
She'd love my dear, new, little friend
Since she has had to go.

So thank you to the Dogs' Home
For my new four-legged friend,
 I've down-sized with my puppy,
And I know that that's the trend!

March 2014

Gabby-Soccer Star

for William and Aisha

I have a little puppy
She really is a trick,
She gets the ball down on the beach,
I have to be so quick.

She'd make a champion goalie;
Her soccer skills are neat;
The only trouble is she thinks that balls
Are really made to eat!

She chews them all into a pulp
And leaves bits on the beach.
She seems to think she knows it all,
She's very hard to teach.

I think she needs a soccer team,
No transfer fees required;
Just pay her fare to Canberra,
She's all you have desired.

She'll block the goal with great aplomb;
No ball will pass her by;
But when she chews the leather up,
The team will shout "You die!"

She even does that little jump
Which goalies often do.
She loves a game and plays along
And you would love her too!

With love from Nanna, May 2014

Gabby on Nutgrove Beach

Gabby's sleeping habits

Every night's a "one-dog night",
For Gabby sleeps with me.
I do not really want her to.
But it's where she wants to be!

She starts on her doggy bed
All snuggled up and warm
But when she sees me settle down,
She's always true to form.

She slithers from her doggy bed
Up towards my shoulder,
Then ruckles up my doona edge
And gradually gets bolder.

She finds an entrance to my bed,
She slides between each sheet
Until she's at the foot of it
And right beside my feet.

She nests there practically all night
Although she'll change her spot.
She sometimes surfaces for air,
I think she gets too hot.

When morning comes and I wake up
She's snuggled there beside me,
Then back she goes inside the bed
If I move her woe betide me!

She rules the roost when I'm asleep,
She succeeds each night,
And I have truly given up;
Though I know it isn't right!

But I admit I do not really mind
This small hot water bottle
But if she hears the slightest sound
Her bark I cannot throttle.

She guards me like a real guard dog
You'd think she had been trained.
She has a huge, alarming bark.
Protection I have gained!

I wonder when the summer comes
If she will still be there
Inside my bed, all snuggled up
Or whether I'll despair

And shut her in the kitchen
And try to keep her out
Or whether once again she'll win?
I don't think there's much doubt!

*Margaret Eldridge, contented owner of
Gabby, adopted from the Dogs' Homes,
Risdon, February 2014*

Gabby's new skill

When Gabby came from you to me
She had some doggy issues,
But now they're mostly sorted out,
Although she still chews tissues!

She's settled down quite well I think;
She loves walks on the beach;
She greets the dogs and owners there
And says g'day to each.

She feared the water lots at first,
But slowly had a wade,
But swim? Now that's another thing
And in her depth she stayed.

She loves her ball it's plain to see
And got it from the river
But if it went beyond her depth
She'd hang about and dither

In and out she'd splash around
But swim, "I'd rather not"
Until one day the ball went out,
She braved it to the spot!

An audience along the shore
Praised my little mate
And told her "What a clever dog!"
And we got home quite late

Because: Gabby saw three handsome ducks
Swimming side by side
And, bless her, she was in like Flynn
And I was filled with pride.

The audience was worried sick.
And prayed her duck would fly,
But no, it swam out to the boats
Safely moored nearby.

The oohs and ahs and "Goodness me's"
As I took off my jacket,
Prepared to swim and rescue her;
When she returned, the racket!

Gabby now shows off her skill,
No hesitation ever;
It's taken easily a year,
But isn't Gabby clever!

Margaret Eldridge, proud owner of Gabby,
adopted from the Dogs' Homes, Risdon, 27th
February 2014

For Emma at Brightside

Minke was adopted from Brightside Rescue Farm at Cygnet. Emma Haswell and her volunteers do a marvellous job, taking in animals of all sorts and helping them find a home. I took Slinky whose name I changed to Minke. There are several rhymes about him as I wanted Emma to be aware of the progress of the quaint, long-haired dachshund she persuaded me to take.

Dear Emma, just a catch up,
I hear you broke your wrist;
This comes to say I'm sorry
And you're well and truly missed.

You made a good decision,
I've landed on my feet,
This home is absolutely fab
And suits me such a treat!

Gabby loves me this I know
Although she rarely shows it;
But that's all right. I love her
And she well and truly knows it.

We curl up on the settee
Or in the garden in the sun;
I wash her face so carefully
Until she's clean and done.

We walk together on the lead,
We're an impressive team,
You'd think we'd been together years
Though things aren't how they seem.

I do a bit of gardening
To help dear Margaret out;
I snuffle out her seedlings
With my elongated snout.

Of course there's still a problem
With my wretched dribbling nose,
But Margaret's quite accepting
Of the problem that I pose.

She always carries tissues
And I'm happy to assist.
I stop and wait. She wipes my nose,
But thinks the problem will persist.

The beach, well that's a story;
I always stayed on lead
But now I'm trained, obedient
And run off lead at speed.

I aim for likely donors
Of doggie treats you see,
They give me some and pat a lot
And tell me that they like me!

Now we have a dog door
Which stays open day and night.
If the neighbour's cat should try it out
He's in for such a fright!

You really wouldn't know me,
I'm quite a different fellow;
I've settled down amazingly;
You might even say I'm mellow!

Except when Margaret leaves me
And then I really howl.
I hate it when she's not around;
I think it's really foul.

When she comes home I raise the roof
Couldn't be more delighted.
I've got her back to hug and love,
Once more we are united.

When Margaret hops onto the bed
To have her nanna nap
She heaves me up to share the space
It's even better than her lap.

I have to say I'm fearsome
When people come to call.
I don't distinguish, known or not
I just bark and growl at all.

But on the whole I'm friendly
Especially if there's a treat
For then I sit discretely
And gobble up and eat.

So if you were a bit concerned
About your choice of home,
Please don't worry. I am fine.
There's no way that I'll roam!

September 2018

Minke Catching Up with Emma

It's some time since we've had a chat.
I thought you'd like to know
What we've been up to here at home,
Sort of from go to woe.

In May my darling mother
Was very, very sick.
The ambos came and wanted
To move her very quick.

I stood my ground when they arrived;
I wouldn't let them in.
I sat right on dear Margaret,
And made a dreadful din.

There were two of them of course
And I was only one,
So off she went to hospital;
The ambo's job was done.

Four days later Mum came home
And we were so excited,
And as for Mum, you'd understand,
She was just delighted.

The months went by and we were fine
Mum was getting stronger.
We were getting back to normal
And the days were getting longer.

And then dear Margaret had a fall
And landed on her shoulder.
The trouble is she doesn't bounce
Now that she's getting older!

Back to hospital again
Her shoulder badly torn,
And that is how it's going to stay
Our Mum is kind of worn!

The shoulder cannot be repaired
But Mum is tough and strong;
Despite it being difficult
She'll find a way to soldier on.

Matin walked us every day
And also gave us food;
He lives down in our chalet
He really is so good.

Gabby and I will help her,
We love her oh so much,
We are a team, a trio,
We provide a caring touch.

Team Eldridge now is rallying;
It may take quite a while,
But lots of folk have offered help
Accepted with a smile.

We get our walk each morning,
Our meals are still on time,
And best of all there's Margaret.
Our life is now sublime!

Greetings to all at Brightside,
We love the Facebook page.
We always press on "like" of course
Despite occasional rage.

Thank goodness you are there dear Emma,
With all that wondrous crew.
Thank you from this trio
For everything you do.

September 2020

Photo courtesy of Janice Luckman, from her painting of Jonas

Jonas' Big Adventure

My Mum went off and left me
With her sister for a while.
They may have thought it A O K
But it didn't make me smile.

The door was opened just in time
For me to run away;
She may be a lovely sister
But I wasn't going to stay!

Sandy Bay's a strange place,
I do not know it well.
Now which direction should I take?
It was really hard to tell.

I headed for the river
But the main road was a puzzle.
Someone tried to stop me
But they couldn't grab my muzzle.

The cars were coming thick and fast,
I hurried up and down,
And then I left the median strip
And headed in to town.

Davey Street is very wide
And busy that's for sure,
So I made my way to Barrack St,
My judgement rather poor.

But what's a little chap to do?
I had to cross the river;
All alone and very scared
I began to shiver.

Meanwhile, my Mum was frantic,
Called family and friends;
Messages were going wild;
I was one of Facebook's trends.

Of course I didn't know it;
I just travelled far and wide,
Wishing hard and praying
To have Janice by my side.

I found myself down by the docks,
Looking for my Mummy;
But one false move and in I fell,
Paddling madly on my tummy.

The water it was freezing
And I'm really not a swimmer,
But I paddled hard as I could go
Though my hopes were getting dimmer.

Someone shouted "See the seal!"
And I kept swimming on.
I really thought my time had come
And I was nearly gone.

And then just in the nick of time
A little boat came by.
People grabbed and wrapped me up
And I began to cry.

Thanks to Jo and Linda
And those people in the boat.
Two days of mad adventure
And an extremely soggy coat!

Hypothermia made me shiver
But I'm really better now.
I've got my Mummy back again
But you'll never know just how!!!

Greyhound Viewing, Kingston Petbarn 7th September 2019

My Mum and I decided
To head to Kingston Town,
To see the Brightside greyhounds,
Though the rain was pouring down.

There they were at Kingston Petbarn
Looking smart and warmly snug
With coats of many colours,
Some dogs curled up on a rug.

When I was down at Brightside
I had several greyhound friends;
They're so big and I'm so small
I think I bucked the trends!

We hoped that we would see you;
I dressed up very smart;
My tag said "Brightside Rescued Me";
I had to play my part!

Our first attempt was failure;
They said you had just left.
I'm not quite sure what Margaret felt
But I think she was bereft!

She really wanted us to meet;
It's been more than a year
Since I moved from Brightside up to town
And left you, Emma dear.

Well, back we went to Petbarn,
To have another try,
And sure enough you turned up,
And Margaret tried hard not to cry.

As you scooped me up into your arms;
I remember well your care.
Each resident at Brightside
Knew that you were there!

I lived there with Longfellow;
He was my dearest mate,
But I heard you whisper, Emma,
That he had met his fate.

He stayed behind there when I left,
But was slowly wearing out;
I think you said "dementia",
But you loved him I've no doubt.

He's gone to Doggie Heaven,
Beyond the rainbow's end
And I have said a little prayer
In remembrance of my friend.

Thank you dearest Emma,
How special that we met;
May all your rescued darlings
Become a much loved pet.

September 2019

Now to the jingles written to raise funds for the Dogs' Homes of Tasmania to whom I owe thanks for my first Tasmanian dog Kiri, Tess and Gabby.

Each Christmas I write a jingle, distribute copies to all the dog walkers on Nutgrove Beach and collect donations.

In 2021 we made $1500 which isn't bad for a jingle! The challenge this year is to raise $2000 and I have issued a challenge to other dog-walking areas to try to do what we do.

The Dogs' Homes will make a video for their social media page, fingers crossed.

Kita   *Gabby*

Welcome back to all of you
Who own the Nutgrove pooches;
And welcome to the dogs themselves,
Especially the smoochers.

At Christmas time we celebrate
And spoil our doggie friends,
But we also think of Dogs' Homes dogs
And try to make amends.

For Dogs' Homes dogs life's not been fun,
They've had their share of troubles
But with the money we collect
Let's turn those into bubbles.

The staff and friends at Risdon Vale
Give love and care each day.
If we can send some cash along
It will help strays on their way.

Nutgrove dogs are lucky dogs,
Their owners take such care,
They walk them on this lovely beach
Which others have to share!

Off the lead 'til 9 am
The dogs have so much fun.
Their owners too enjoy it all,
Until their time is done.

There's breeds galore who walk this beach,
And many backgrounds here;
As well as pedigrees and all
There's mixtures never fear!

There's border collies, lots of them,
Dalmatians, daschunds slim,
Labs, retrievers, beagles too
And shnauzers with neat trim.

There's one great dane so stately,
Spaniels (King Charles and others)
And lots of little fluff-balls
And some with dubious mothers!

There's some which have to stay on lead
For fear they'll not come back
And others quite obsessed with balls
That keep them well on track.

And quite a few are Dogs' Homes dogs
And yes we love them truly.
Of course we've had to train them up
For some were quite unruly!

But now they've learnt a thing or two
And Nutgrove is their beach.
So happy Christmas to them all
And greetings to you each.

Our dogs are loved and walked and fed.
It's like that at the Dogs' Home
And when it's time for them to leave,
They won't be strays who roam.

Forever homes we hope are found
With owners kind who care,
And all donations that we give
Mean we have done our share.

Penny rang from Victoria,
Said "I really like your sign.
Can I show it to our council?
Can you send it me on line?

I'll send you a donation
For Hobart Dogs' Homes dogs;"
And the Homes said our Dogs' Breakfast
Will be up there on their blogs.

So you see the word is spreading;
Nutgrove could start a trend
Of breakfasts for the canines
And the owners they befriend.

What would we do without them,
Each precious, loving pet?
The difference they've made to our lives,
We never will forget.

So here's to dogs and friendship.
We owe them such a lot.
On Nutgrove Beach they love us too.
It is their favourite spot.

Jingles and Me by Margaret Eldridge AM

Nutgrove for the Dogs' Homes

This has been a dreadful year,
Whatever can I say?
We've watched as others suffered
Every single day.

Covid's like the devil,
Affecting all we know;
We pray a vaccination
Will help make Covid go.

One thing which makes us thankful,
Our dog have stood the test;
They've kept us sane through lockdown,
They really are the best.

And now Christmas approaches
We think of other pets
Especially at the Dogs' Homes
Where we know of costs and debts.

It's expensive minding pooches
That don't have a loving home.
They're taking in so many strays
For dogs are prone to roam.

You have an opportunity
To help the Dogs' Homes pets
And raise some cash this Christmas,
It's as easy as it gets.

Just give me cash, don't argue,
And you will get a rhyme,
And I will write the Dogs' Homes
A cheque at Christmas time.

Our dogs are loved and treasured,
They worship us we know,
They even love each other;
If there's treats then they're not slow.

We've lost some doggy friends this year
And that's been hard and sad,
We're thankful for their friendship
And all the fun we've had.

If you come down to Nutgrove
You'll meet our special friends;
There's many different types and breeds
And you may even notice trends.

It used to be the schnauzers
Who seemed to rule the roost,
But now there's lots of dachshunds
That have received a little boost.

Collies, well there's plenty,
Black and white and brown,
Labradoodles, hounds and spaniels
And the smartest dogs in town.

Shepherds, bulldogs, vizsla,
Husky, Airedale, corgi too
Jack Russels and other terriers,
Pugs and furry fluffballs all know what to do.

You'll see greyhounds, marrema, beagles,
Retrievers, Labrador
Irish terriers and setters
And many, many more.

Not all the dogs are purebred,
That's very clear to see,
Rather dubious parentage
Is obvious to me.

Staffy crosses, mixtures,
Dogs both large and small,
The main thing is we love them
And they all have a ball.

Can we exceed the total
Of what we raised last year?
Let's try $1000
We can do it, never fear.

Thanks to the Dogs' Homes carers,
Good luck to all out there;
The funds we raise this Christmas
Will show we really care

Dec 2020

That festive time of year has come
When I remind you all
I'm collecting for the Dogs' Homes;
I'll take gifts both large and small.

I'll try to mention every breed
We see on Nutgrove Beach;
I know that you'll remind me
If success I do not reach!

Let's start with labradoodles
And of course, the mixtured poodles
There's several combinations,
In fact you know, there's oodles!

Spaniels are back in fashion
Some black and white or tan,
And Cavalier King Charles of course
And they have many a fan.

The mini schnauzers used to be
The most prolific seen,
But others may be catching up,
Can you see what I mean?

Dachshund numbers have increased
With fur both short and long.
They really are the strangest shape.
Their design I think is wrong!

Retrievers, Labradors abound
Golden, black and brown;
Dependable and cheerful
Favourites around town.

One very stately Maremmar
With coat so very pale.
She came from the Dogs' Homes
Out at Risdon Vale.

One sheepdog looks like Lassie
Such a lovely creature,
And just one big bull mastiff.
Its strength is quite a feature.

There are several staffie purebreds
And staffie crosses, quite a few.
If you want to check their parentage,
I have not got a clue!

There's hounds and several pointers
Weimaraner and a rottie,
I'm petrified I've missed a breed,
Who says kelpies can be dotty?

Chihuahua types and furballs
Play on Nutgrove Beach,
But some dogs have to stay on lead
Or they'd soon be out of reach.

German Shepherds, collies,
Which try to catch the waves
Or chase the seagulls, barking.
Plenty of close shaves!

Greyhounds have been rescued
From the racing track,
It wasn't safe or humane
And now they're giving back.

Bulldogs, there are several sorts,
Big and small and stocky
And then an aged Highland White
And you know his name is Lauchie.

Terriers of many types,
Irish, silky, Yorkshire and Jack Russel
Bedlington, corgi and dalmatian
Join the doggie bustle.

Let's not forget the beagles
Who sniff along the beach,
They should be at the airport,
Where drugs could be in reach.

The vizslas, boxer and Airedale
Have fun and race about;
Hounds and several pointers
Are joining in no doubt!

There's puppies with high energy
And several sedate oldies,
But whether old or young you know
Everyone's a goldie.

We can't forget the bitsers
Of one sort or another,
Parentage is dubious,
Check their father and their mother!

God Bless the doggie friends we've lost,
They gave us of their best,
We never will forget them,
May they enjoy their rest.

So how about it Nutgrove walkers,
Can we raise a lot of cash?
We've reached 1000 twice before.
I don't think that's too rash!

Donations to Margaret (with Gabby and Minke) on the beach, or in her letterbox at 43 Maning Ave.

Dogs' Homes Christmas Fundraiser 2022

As Christmas time approaches
It's time for the Dogs' Homes jingle
And I must print and distribute it
Where Nutgrove dog-walkers mingle.

Last year we raised a tidy sum.
Can we do even better?
The challenge is $2000
When you receive this letter!

As usual I will try my best
To mention every breed
But don't be cross dear walkers,
If I do not succeed.

Let's start with all the bitsers,
Those with parentage unsure,
I have one, my darling Gabby
And I know there are lots more!

There's been a noted increase
In dachshunds over time,
And one of them's my other dog,
Dear Minke's past his prime.

Our dogs are so important,
We could not do without
Each wagging tail of friendship
And each inquisitive snout!

There's corgis too and Schnauzers,
Miniature of course,
And many poodle crossses
From a different source.

They range from white and fluffy,
Through tan to darkest black.
There are so many of them,
 They make a joyous pack!

Collies, energetic,
Race on Nutgrove Beach
But gulls and plovers by the score,
Stay still and out of reach!

Spaniels too of all kinds,
Mostly King Charles the cavalier type.
Will they become more popular
With all the King Charles hype?

Terriers are lively
And we have got all sorts;
Cheeky little pooches
And always such good sports.

Chihuahuas dash around quite fast;
Labs and retrievers splash.
They love the water at Nutgrove
And race in at a dash.

There's a sheepdog looks like Lassie
Walks along quite stately.
Hey, that just reminds me,
I haven't seen it lately.

Hounds and pointers, several
Run on Nutgrove beach,
Greyhounds who've been rescued
Far from the racetrack's reach.

There's a couple handsome beagles.
They sniff along the beach.
Smell is so important
But things get out of reach.

There are several purebred staffies,
Powerful dogs for sure,
And Highland whites and scotties.
And I'm sure there are lots more.

I know there is an Airedale.
Who pinches other's toys;
And kelpies fast and furious
Gorgeous little boys.

I must remember vizslas
A boxer and whippet too
A German Shepherd and a bulldog.
And that will have to do.

We have a three-legged wonder;
You really cannot tell.
It races round like others
And balances so well.

We've lost some much-loved friends this year
The farewells make us sad.
They leave a gap that's hard to fill,
Those dog friends that we had.

Thanks to those at Risdon
Who care for all the strays,
And those that are surrendered
And have seen better days.

A challenge now to others
To help the Dogs' Homes cope.
For if you can you will be
Giving unwanted dogs some hope.

Bring some cash dear walkers
Don't say you haven't any,
The Dogs' Homes dogs deserve a treat
For there are oh, so many.

Cash to Margaret Eldridge on the beach or in her letterbox at 43 Maning Avenue, Sandy Bay.

Memo to City of Hobart

We have found that Hobart City Council responds much more quickly and pays attention when I write a jingles asking for action!

We saw your advert in the Merc,
And were somewhat confused;
Dogs on Nutgrove 6-10 pm
Had us quite bemused!

Roaming in the gloaming
With other doggie friends?
Not quite sure what message
Your advert really sends!

I gather you want comments;
Well this is mine for sure.
I was happy with the other ad
Which gave us one hour more.

Some time ago I'd asked you
For help when dark and cold.
It isn't just the dogs you know;
Some walkers are quite old!

So now I think it's sorted out:
It was a Mercury typo,
No need to worry any more
Or panic with a hypo.

Winters will be easier
For the walkers and dog friends,
And we are very happy
Approving latest trends.

We're glad you see it just like us;
Nutgrove's a paradise
For dogs of all varieties
And we all think that's nice.

Thank you Hobart City,
Aldermen and Lord Mayor.
Come and visit Nutgrove
And see what we do there!

Cormorants aplenty,
Gulls of many sorts,
Dolphins frolicking away
And seals, they are such sports.

Yatchs, canoes and dinghies
Make use of Nutgrove Beach,
And I for one am happy
That it's all within my reach.

The social interaction
At the beginning of my day
Improves my mood and builds my health
In a very special way.

My dogs and I all benefit
We're down there without fail
Even when it's raining
Or blowing up a gale.

It really is an asset
For folks both young and old
And canine friends of every sort;
It's worth its weight in gold!

And just a word of thanks again
For your employees on the beach,
Who clear up stuff and manage
The things we cannot reach!

Thank you Hobart City Council

I didn't sleep a wink last night
So changed my daily walk.
My dogs were really quite confused
And watched me like a hawk.

Nutgrove is where we wander,
Usually at eight,
But today we didn't make it,
And were considerably late!

But due to recent changes
(Off lead from 9-10)
Our rather late arrival
Just didn't matter then!

Gabby played the usual ball,
Minke followed on,
And there was quite a different group,
My regulars long gone.

We dog-walkers are a special group,
Beach minders through and through.
We pick up rubbish, keep an eye
And do what we can do.

We'd like to thank the council
For that welcomed extra hour.
For us it's made a difference,
Your response to people power!

September 2019

HCC Please Take Note!

The sand which leaves the beach,
Wherever does it go?
Dear Hobart City Council,
We think that you should know.

The entry place to Nutgrove
Which goes from Beechworth Road
Demonstrates the problem
Just look! A sandy load.

You've put a brush at one end,
Thank you and well done,
But we need one there at Beechworth
It could actually be some fun!

It just might be quite good you know,
As we line up for our turn,
Meeting folk and chatting,
There's such a lot to learn!

The sand is on the pathway,
Diminishing the beach,
It spreads back on the laneway
As far as it can reach.

A brush down at the beach end
Would help us all to leave
Accumulated beach sand,
Well that's what we believe.

Dear Hobart City Council
Please listen to us all.
A brush right there to clean our shoes
And we can have a ball!

What do you think dear alderfolk,
Can you accommodate our plea?
We dare not hold on to our breath,
We'll have to wait and see!

From the Nutgrove Beach lovers.
November 2020

Nutgrove Pontoon

We really want our pontoon back;
You promised we would get it.
You said that it would be replaced.
We'd like to see you let it.

You said that it might take a while
And what a while we've waited!
Time has passed and now it's months
That we've waited with breath baited!

The swimmers have nowhere to go,
They just make for the boats.
There's nowhere there to take a rest,
On a real pontoon that floats.

There's been a pontoon at our beach
For nigh on eighty years.
You can't destroy our history
So cancel all our fears.

The cormorants have flown away;
They've found another perch
But we like them feel HCC
Has left us in the lurch.

We have sneaky feeling
Nutgrove's the poor relation
And Long Beach supersedes our spot
Which feeds our consternation.

You say the engineers will meet
And have a consultation
But how long can it really take
To do this restoration?

So bring it back; there's no excuse;
The buoys still mark the spot.
Don't think we'll take this lying down;
Or we'll not trust you lot!!!

Margaret Eldridge March 2016

For Ray

Back on Nutgrove Beach, we had a lovely dog-walking friend called Ray Friend and when he died his daughter asked if I would write something for his funeral, I felt a jingle was not appropriate and so I wrote the following which I read in his memory. Some of the dog walkers were present and a number of strangers, members of Ray's family and friends, were very happy at how we acknowledged him.

Ray was a friend
By name and by nature,
Not a bosom pal,
Not an intimate,
But he was our friend.

We met him on the beach;
Our dogs made introductions,
Louis a little reserved
Fiercely loyal and never far away,
But Ray was our friend.

If you walk your dog on Nutgrove,
You may just understand
The pleasure and affinity
Of the dog-walking folk
For our friend Ray

Proud of his precious family
He dearly loved each one,
And introduced us to them
Sometimes sitting on the wall,
For Ray was our friend.

We grieved for Ray when Mary died,
His life companion and his love;
It was not the same without her,
We felt the enormous loss
To our friend Ray.

A cup of tea with Ray
Lasted quite a while
For stories came with tea
And what tales he could tell,
Our friend Ray.

Tales of when a young man
He fished in the far north,
Of a life in exotic places;
Boats and ships had meaning
For our friend Ray

Sometimes just a smile
And then a quick good morning,
Hiding how he struggled
But never a complaint
From our friend Ray

As Parkinsons took its toll
He needed all his strength
To walk the length of Nutgrove
With sticks so bravely held
By our friend Ray

A gentleman was Ray.
Courteous to the last.
We admired his determination
And the valiant way he coped,
Our friend Ray.

"I only saw him last week"
They said along the beach;
We're thankful that the end
Was such a quick release
For our friend Ray.

Nutgrove will be the poorer
Without our dear friend Ray.
He's walking on another beach
Surrounded by our high regard.
For dear Ray Friend.

Margaret Eldridge and the Nutgrove dog-walkers and friends,

July 2017

Re-Cycling

The dog-walkers are a caring community and we kept each other sane during lock-down. When Miles broke his leg early in 2022, there was much sympathy and concern.

Dear Miles we're sad to hear you fell,
And that you broke your leg.
Just remember won't you that
A leg's a crucial peg!

Maddy's fine and bouncy,
Nothing slows her down!
She misses you I am quite sure,
Just thinks you're out of town.

Tessa, well she's lonely
And very worried too,
But let's be realistic,
There's not much she can do!

When you were just a baby
You crawled then learned to walk.
This time round will be much harder;
It cannot be just talk!

Up and at'em Miles dear friend,
Show those medics how
Your strong determination
Will surely kick in now!

Absence makes the heart grow fonder.
Tessa will survive.
Just shelve the bike for a week or two,
And avoid another dive!

6.3.2022 Margaret, for your concerned dog-walking friends.

Health is the greatest gift,
Contentment the greatest wealth,
Faithfulness the best relationship.

Buddha

Photo courtesy of Ellyse Tran and Tri Tri Tran, from Ellyse (aged 16)'s sketch.

Jingles on a Health theme, my own and others!

Cataract 1 April 2004

How could I have forgotten

The intensity of Autumn colours,

The detail of bark on eucalyptus trees,

The settlements across the Derwent

And the startling contrast of black and white?

The blurred outlines now carefully defined,

The depth of vision has returned.

The distant hills and purple headed mountain

Are mine once more to savour and enjoy.

With surgeon's skill and grace divine

These joys and more have been restored.

Photo courtesy of Ellyse Tran and Tri Tri Tran,
from Ellyse (aged 11)'s sketching book.

Pretty Pink

Pink to make the boys wink,
Was what my grandma said.
She'd made my dress in pretty pink
Instead of blue or red!

My neighbour asked "And how are you?"
And I replied "I'm fine.
I'm fit and well and in the pink,
I am not in decline"!

I'm sure you've heard of pinking shears
That cut a frilly edge.
I keep mine in my sewing box,
It's up there on the ledge.

I guess you know the flowers called pinks,
With perfume sweet and heady.
In cottage gardens they abound,
Aroma at the ready.

And we all have a pinky,
Right here as you can see.
Refined and genteel ladies
Hold it so when drinking tea!

Then there's the pink we wear today,
To acknowledge a disease
That can wreak havoc when it strikes
And causes much unease.

There are victims of this illness
Whose memory strong we hold,
But here's to the survivors
And researchers' trials bold.

The funds we raise in this pink way
Will one day find a cure,
So dig in deep and help the cause:
BREAST CANCER GONE FOR SURE.

October 28th 2011

The Return of the Kerrie!

Our Kerrie's back amongst us
With knees all shiny new,
She's a real bionic woman,
Just one of quite a few.

Her joints were truly awful,
She very near despaired.
The surgeon said "No worries girl,
I'll soon have you repaired!"

With nurses at the ready
And instruments galore,
He removed the offending knee joints,
And replaced them from his store!

There's not much left to reconstruct
That's not been done before;
And Kerrie says she's had enough,
"I don't want any more!"

But all that's now behind her,
She's struggled back to life,
Battled crutches, sticks and
All the associated strife.

While you've been convalescing
We've not known what to do,
For counting aqua numbers
Was always up to you.

With knees that function really well
The world's her oyster true.
There'll be no holding Kerrie back,
So many things to do.

The question now arises,
So will you answer please;
It's "When will you come back to aqua
With your brand new titanium knees?

Margaret Eldridge,
Dr Syntax lunch April 2012.

On Being a Wuss!

I admire you Dr Pritchard,
You've cared for me so well,
But that cortisone injection
Really made me yell!

It hit the spot I have to say
And I was quite impressed,
But two hours later the pain was back
And I was quite distressed.

I know you think that I'm a wuss;
That really isn't true;
I've dealt with pain for years and years.
As many valiant troopers do.

I suffered migraine early on
Til I turned seventy-five;
I wonder now just how I coped
With kids and job, and thrived.

Stress fractures in my lower spine
Said surgery was needed
But I went to aquarobics,
And the surgeon, he conceded.

My breasts have crazy paving
From all the ops I've had
To take out lumps and suchlike.
Thank goodness they weren't bad.

Have you ever been through childbirth?
I've done it once, twice, thrice.
The pain is worth it in the end
But it isn't really nice!

My gall bladder got up to tricks
It was excruciating
And when I had the thing removed,
It was debilitating.

In Java many moons ago
Dengue was the trouble
They call it break-bone fever
And it really burst my bubble.

And then I had that awful fall
That jarred all of my body,
No-one stopped to help me
And I thought that was shoddy.

Dark in night-time Melville St.,
The cars went rushing by.
All I could do was shout out loud
Til someone heard my cry.

Osteo is never fun,
It's bothered me quite badly;
I've had new toes and thumbs of course,
And a new hip I had gladly.

But sadly now it's damaged;
It was a nasty fall.
I wish it would return to health,
But I regret that isn't all.

The kidneys are not happy.
I didn't take as much
As different doctors had prescribed,
As pills I rarely touch.

A month ago I hurt my back
Lifting Minke in the car
I felt it "go" as I bent down ,
It really made me jar.

The dogs were happy on the bed
Instead of having walks.
For two whole days they snuggled up.
We had some lovely talks

The rest has made a wondrous change.
I think I will recover.
The painful hip is almost right
As you will now discover.

It must have been the rest I had,
Lolling on the bed.
Rest is the solution
Dr Google said.

So wuss or not I'm walking well
Just checking what you think,
But all of me feels better.
I'm almost "in the pink".

February 2019

For Avance and the team at Calvary 22 9 2017

Anaesthetics aren't my thing,
They've always been a bane,
But when my hip had been replaced
I actually woke up sane!

No little men around the room,
No curtains flapping madly,
No High BP or vomiting
That treated be so badly!

This time they finally got it right.
I woke as from a dream.
I'm very grateful to you all-
You are a wondrous team.

But one stands out especially.
That dark Zimbabwean face.
His smile so big I won't forget
That he was on my case!

He greeted me, we chatted,
We talked about his land.
I really want to thank him;
His being there was grand.

I'm now bionic woman.
Mike Pritchard's fixed my hip;
I'm walking well with crutches
Taking great care not to slip.

I trek along the corridor,
New hip first step each time.
My crutches lent by Helen
Didn't cost a dime!

The family's been to see me,
To check and bring me treats.
I guess they're pretty happy
I'm back on my two feets!

I do my exercises,
I've showered and used the loo.
I've plastered on the arnica
And done all I should do.

At 10 tomorrow I can leave
And sleep in my own bed
With Holly there to care for me
I hope I'll be well fed!

22 9 2017

Bionic Folk (For Michael Pritchard, November 2017)

Bionic folk are very pleased a surgeon took us on;
With hips and knees which let us down,
Our aching joints are gone!

New ones we have to help us walk,
They serve us very well.
They're miracles of surgery
(Though time alone will tell!)

And who's the man we have to thank
For joints that do not taint?
His name is Michael Pritchard-
A surgeon and a saint!

So thank you dear St Michael,
The patron saint of joints.
We're glad you got your hatchets out
And fixed us at all points!

*Best friends are the people in your life
who make you laugh louder,
smile brighter and live better.*

Unknown

When I started writing jingles for my Aqua group, I would share them at our Christmas and mid-year lunches.

Kerrie suggested that instead of just performing them and dishing out free copies, I use the jingles as a fund-raiser and ask for a donation for Motor Neurone Disease Research which is a cause close to my heart as I explained earlier.

We have raised thousands of dollars this way and I am grateful to Kerrie for her suggestion. There are other jingles associated with friendships made at Aqua classes.

The Water Babies

We're called the Water Babies,

Deep water is our spot;

We exercise with vigour,

But tend to talk a lot.

We love our aqua workout,

We tackle it with zest,

Cross country skis and stomach crunch,

And dumb-bells at our chest.

We sprint around the dive pool,

We set a cracking pace;

We like to think we do it

With elegance and grace!

Star jumps and rock and rolling

Are well within our range;

We do the routine actions,

But rather like a change.

Through many years of aqua

Instructors come and go;

We've weathered storms together

But you really wouldn't know.

We're young at heart and cheerful,

We're here come rain or shine;

The Aquatic Centre's faithfuls,

And we know we're doing fine!

June 2004

Aqua Christmas 2007

I did not write a poem,
Or another Christmas rhyme.
If you lot want my verses
You must ask me in good time.

My mind is full of other things,
I don't know which is worse –
A thesis to be handed in
Or another Christmas verse!

It's not that I don't love you,
That's really not the case.
It's just that time is running out;
I can't keep up the pace.

I had a dream of heaven.
The aqua group was there.
St Peter donned his aqua belt
Midst angels bright and fair.

And God said "Well, how pleased I am
You're here, your heavenly place.
Please teach us all the aqua moves
And liven heaven's space."

The angels, they did aqua flies,
The cherubs frog-jumped proud,
And you and I, in aqua mode,
Did star jumps on a cloud.

My dream is done and so am
It really is a pity
This offering at Drysdale House
Is such a silly ditty!

So Happy Christmas aqua folk,
Our fun must never cease.
My greetings at this festive time
For a New Year filled with peace.

Aqua Class Christmas Do at Drysdale

Christmas comes but once a year,
We learned that rhyme at school.
But we have Christmas every time
We jump into the pool!

Our aqua group is oh such fun,
We pull our belts on tight.
The water's often rather cold;
They never get it right!

We like it in the diving pool,
The water's pretty deep.
Instructors run along the side
And we respond like sheep!

"Let's do our star jumps strong and wide"
Ray's very keen on these.
He has us touching all four walls
And touching hands to knees.

Dear Donna says "Five seconds more,
Egg-beater arms and legs;
Let's get your heart-beat right up high"
She very nearly begs!

Now Toni runs a cracking class,
She sure keeps up the pace.
She winds us up, pulls out all stops;
The strain shows on each face!

Young Sita's an enthusiast.
We think she's taking pills
That keep her bouncing up and down
And give us aqua thrills!

There's Andrew. He's the sort of lad
Who keeps us all committed.
His classes draw a lively crowd
And feedback is permitted!

A new instructor came along
And said "My name is Mel".
She has a plan of fast, relax.
It seems to suit us well!

Another aqua Jingle, Christmas 2006

The clock up on the wall is ours,
We got it when we nagged.
It didn't work for months and months
As no-one could be fagged.

The classes are for young and old,
We turn up rain or shine.
We want to keep our bodies fit,
The exercise is fine.

The bodies vary as you know.
Some are a little fatter.
But here today at Drysdale House
Calories do not matter!

... Because
We'll all be back at aqua class.
We'll rock and roll with vigour.
We'll wag our tongues and exercise,
Attack the flab with rigour.

Our thanks go out to staff and friends
For keeping us together;
For making sure we all work out
Regardless of the weather.

So Happy Christmas one and all,
But don't forget your figure,
While eating all the Christmas fare
Your figure could get bigger!

You'll have to all come back next year
To Tatts Aquatic Centre.
So raise your glasses, noodles and dumb-bells,
To 2007's aqua adventure.

Christmas 2008

Helen came and visited
Stan and Annie too
And several others rang me up
Good wishes to renew.

"Now mind you come to Drysdale House,
Our luncheon's on again.
The gang will all be there you know.
Just disregard the pain!"

How could I miss this special day?
Our annual Christmas luncheon.
No matter that my innards feel
They've battled with a truncheon!

Enough of me. It's Christmas time
And time for celebration.
The food is good, eat up and drink.
Don't overdo libation!

What would we do without our class?
The trainers and the members;
The friendship and the jollity
Acknowledged in Decembers.

We'd miss the frigid diving pool,
The exercise (and chatter!)
The trainers with their 3,2,1s
And other things that matter.

Murray Rivers, star jumps wide
And rock and rolls to follow.
We're forced along at cracking pace
With barely time to swallow.

"Touch all four walls", then froggy jumps,
(Make sure you all croak "rivett")
It makes instructors' days you know
And doesn't hurt to give it.

"Sit on a chair, just use your arms.
Grab dumb-bells (maybe noodles).
Don't stop, keep up intensity"
They think we're left with oodles!

Breast stroke arms and flutter kicks
And stomach crunches furious
Sustained by thoughts of getting in
To showers so luxurious.

I could go on and list it all
But time is of the essence,
So thanks to Stan who planned today
And graced lunch with his presence.

A Happy Christmas one and all,
May peace, love, joy abound,
And please ensure you're back next year
With aqua friends around.

December 2008

Aqua Christmas Lunch 2009

Marvellous Monday was what Jo said,
And I thought to myself, that's true,
Wonderful Wednesday, Fabulous Friday,
The best days of the week for us too.

For aqua we know is a powerful thing,
Our bodies respond to it well,
We stretch and turn, we bend and we float,
It's the best exercise we can tell.

At aqua we meet a fabulous group
Of friends and acquaintances too,
And instructors who lead us to limits unknown
They're enthusiasts, all of the crew.

Some of us "aquaed" for twenty plus years,
We were members of Dockside then,
But our classes have always lacked one thing,
An equivalent number of men!

But Stan has never let the girls down,
And to our delight we can see
He's been joined by some truly champion blokes,
And sometimes there's more than three!

Now what brings the men to classes like ours?
It must be the aqua chicks,
And the exercise that strengthens them up
And gives an adrenalin fix.

A year of activity, energy plus
Has nearly come to an end.
We've rocked and rolled and bicycled round,
Done Irish jigs with a friend.

Star jumps and frog jumps and YMCAs,
We've fervently done as we're told,
And none of us will ever admit,
That we're gradually getting old!

No Way! We are all truly young at heart,
And aqua will keep us that way,
As we move to the beat and exercise hard,
Slim and sylph-like and trim we will stay!

So here we all are at the Drysdale lunch,
It's Christmas, or soon it will come.
We're here to share with our aqua friends,
There's fifty or more and then some!

We hope that Christmas will bring happiness
And replenish us all with good cheer;
That 2010 will bring peace and success,
And we'll make it to aqua next year!

For aqua we know will improve our health,
It will strengthen our muscles and all,
So here's to aqua 2010,
When we know we will all have a ball!

Aqua Lunch at Wrest Point

I thought I'd take Christmas off
And wouldn't write a ditty
But Helen said "You can't do that,
It would be such a pity!

And when I thought of MND
And how the ditties help them.
I thought of all the cheques I write
And all the cash you've paid them!

I realised then I had to write
A Christmas rhyme this season
To celebrate the aqua year.
There is no better reason!

And what a year we have all had
With aqua classes booming
And people prancing around with sticks.
I see disaster looming!

And yet aficionados say
The sticks are fun to work out.
They build your muscles, help your heart
And strengthen bits that jerk out!

I still need to be convinced
That I won't hurt my frame,
Of worse, won't drown within the pool
With cords and belts to blame.

Are you like me? You dare not miss
For if you do you'll suffer.
Withdrawal symptoms aren't much fun
The next class will be tougher!

If anyone is feeling down
When to the pool they come
Laughs and friendship cheer them up
For sure there's always some.

We benefit in many ways
As in the pool we frolic.
We move in rhythms right and left
The movements are bucolic.

We have instructors tried and true
They work us through and through,
They go to courses, learn new skills
It's great the stuff they do!

And we reward them every time.
We do just what they say.
But sad to say we chatter too.
But then that is our way!

The interaction we enjoy,
It keeps us bright and happy.
We're multi-skilled, two things at once
We're nothing if not snappy.

It's good to see that Helen's here.
She fell and broke her ankle.
She's had some help from other folk
But broken ankles rankle!

Jane too was badly in the wars
When falling at the golf course.
Her pelvis suffered and some ribs,
The pain was felt with force.

It's great to share this Christmas lunch
With aqua friends we treasure.
Our classes offer lots of fun
And pleasure beyond measure.

So thank you all for being here
To celebrate the season.
Make sure you're back at aqua class
Because there is a reason.

Aqua keeps us on our toes.
Not literally you know.
But full of vim and vigour too
It's THE best way to go.

Happy Christmas one and all
And greetings for New Year
We'll make a splash and cut a dash
When we return, no fear.

Travel makes one modest.

You see what a tiny place you occupy in the world.

Gustave Flaubert

We used to have a bugger-off lunch when those heading to the mainland or overseas to avoid the Tasmania winter, were about to depart. Here are a couple samples followed by a jingle written when I went to Nova Scotia to visit Rosie and Mike who spent half the year in Luneburg in their home there. Their historic home there had once belonged to the town cobbler. I was moved to write about this Mr Knox too.

Margaret in Russia!

That Time of Year

That time of year has come around
When some of us are leaving.
To those who stay and 'hold the fort,'
I hope you won't be grieving!

Rose and Mike have made their way
To Lunenburg, you'll pardon.
But not before the floods removed
A large part of their garden.

And Stan will soon be UK bound,
With Matthew, Scott and Ned.
Just what they'll do I cannot guess.
It's better lelt unsaid!

Chris and Gary are journeying too,
They really love to travel.
Where they go and who they see
In time they will unravel.

I too am off again this year.
My daughter's now in London.
I'll pack my bags and catch the plane,
And hope they don't get undone!

I'll kiss my grandkids, little dears,
I'll visit friends and rellies.
I'll dash around on underground,
You've seen it on your tellies.

I'll go to see my college friends,
Who're now like me, much older
Than when we chased the college boys;
Those days when we were bolder!

My school friends have arranged a date,
We'll gather for a natter
For though they're poms, they're just like
You, and do enjoy to chatter.

I'll go to Paris, ooh la la!
I feel Champs Elisée beckon.
I'll have a look at the Eiffel tower
It's absolument superbe I reckon!

I'll visit with my French host dad
Who's ninety-seven shortly.
I first went there when I was twelve,
Before I got so portly!

I'm going on a little cruise
Around about in Venice.
I've heard the gondoliers and such
Can really be a menace!

But I am going well prepared.
I've lined my bag with fly wire.
So if thieves try to steal my stuff.
They'll be for the high wire!

We travellers brave will miss you all.
You are our Aqua buddies.
We love you all, yes every one,
There really are no duddies!

Please keep the pool temp nice and warm
And trainers on their toes.
Before you know it we'll be back
Reporting travelling woes!

Delayed flights, lost bags,
Customs checks, is it worth the trouble?
You bet it is, we'll have such fun
You'll never burst our bubble!

So for the white it's au revoir,
We'll really miss our classes.
Let's check I've got my walking stick
And hearing aids and glasses!

Margaret Eldridge May 2011

Lunenburg

Photo courtesy of Minh Hien and Farshid

I had a sense of déja vue
When off the plane I came.
Though Halifax, 'twas Rose and Mike
And they were just the same!

I planned to get the ferry here,
So the internet I check.
But just my luck, the ferry's gone,
So I flew here, what the heck!

I caught a plane in Portland, Maine,
And travelled to Toronto.
By chance, my luggage was left behind
And was not delivered pronto!

So, Rosie's clothes I borrowed then,
They fitted like a glove.
Mike's smart T-shirt sure looked good.
I returned them all with love!

It's great to be in Lunenburg,
I've heard so much about it,
It far exceeds my wildest dreams.
Why ever did I doubt it?

There's lots to do in Lunenburg
With Rose and Mike my hosts,
And when I'm back in Hobart town,
I'll be the one who boasts!

The quaint, bright coloured houses,
Museums more than one.
The horse called John who did his bit,
And "Glimpses", that was fun.

The food kept coming all the time,
Chowder, crabs and scallops.
And ice-cream served with cream on top
And caramel sauce in dollops!

It's just as well I'm moving on,
I fear my girth has risen.
I'll have to curb my appetite
And eat as if in prison!

So thank you both for having me
You're so generous, Rosie, Mike.
I'm off on Thursday, Paris bound
Providing there's no strike!

The Cobbler of Lunenburg

In Prince St. here in Lunenburg
The village cobbler worked.
He was a farmer also,
But chores he never shirked.
"Cobbler, cobbler, mend my shoe,
Get it done by half past two,
Do it neat and do it strong
And I will pay you when it's done."

The cobbler's name was Mr Knox,
'Twas here he plied his trade.
And many folk in Lunenburg
Had shoes to be remade.
Refrain
Herr Zwicker said his feet got wet,
For in his shoes a hole
Stretched from his toes right to his heel
And surely took its toll.
Refrain
A farmer's shoes were very worn
From tramping on the land;
But Mr Knox prepared his tools
And took repairs in hand.
Refrain.
Young Gretel Karst, a maiden sweet,
Had dancing pumps to wear.
The mice had nibbled into them.
And that produced a tear.

Refrain.

A boy from the Academy was kicking stones one day,
Ripped his shoes, not just a scuff;
His father had to pay.
Refrain.
The mayor in busy Lunenburg
Had shoes which needed mending,
He pleaded "Mr Knox I pray,
I need them by week's ending."
Refrain.
Trooper Jack wore army boots
Somewhat the worse for wear;
"Oblige me Mr Knox" he said
"And smarten up this pair."
Refrain.
A bridle from a farmer's horse
Had worn and frayed quite badly.
Mr Knox said "Come back next week.
I'm far too busy, sadly!"
Refrain
So thanks to Mr Knox the cobbler,
Sometimes farming in his field,
But making sure that Lunenburg
Would always be well-heeled!
Refrain.

Photo courtesy of Ellyse Tran and Tri Tri Tran, from Ellyse (aged 16)'s sketch.

It's That Time Again!

Can it really be a year
Since Rose and Mike departed
For Lunenburg, their other home,
And now again they've started!

Nova Scotia calls out strong
And Lunenburg's a treasure.
Friends there will be out in force
To welcome them with pleasure.

Mind you, the time is soon to come
When up will go the "sold" board.
Historic house, shoemaker's shop
They'll leave, though much adored.

Then they will have to stay with friends
When for Canada they hanker.
Meanwhile, Taroona still is theirs;
It's where they've tossed their anchor!

We'll see them back when northern chills
And snow and ice grow thicker;
And we'll be waiting in the pool,
Behind our hands we'll snicker ...

They liven up our aqua class;
We watch them both canoodle.
While we've got dumbbells at the fore,
Or maybe just a noodle.

So off you go, our gourmet friends,
Have fun, enjoy the summer,
While most of us are winter bound,
We hope it's not a bummer.

You Put Your Right Leg In...

Some years ago the aquatic staff
Chose to offer aid
To those who clearly loved the pool
But could not make the grade.

A great machine arrived in style
And really did the trick.
A group of people tried it out
And got in the water quick!

It saved a lot of effort
For those who are less able,
And we were very grateful
The machine made some more stable.

So now you'll understand I'm sure
Why we are quite distressed;
The machine is often out of use
Making us depressed.

Surely you can fix it
YOU thought we needed it
And having had its use
We miss the benefit.

So come on, pull your socks up;
The steps are sharp and rough
The railing wobbles badly
And climbing out is tough.

You scrape your skin and struggle
And need some extra care;
The steps are really tricky
For some who aqua there.

And don't forget the others
Who soon may need the aid
For it's a better way for sure
Than feeling quite afraid.

We really need our aqua
It's crucial to our health
Please keep us in the water,
It's more valuable than wealth.

August 2018

Keeping Abreast July 2019

Colleen is an angel
Who performs a menial task
When we are in the change room,
And I never have to ask.

With a rather painful shoulder
It's very hard for me
To do the hooks up on my bra
As anyone can see.

But Colleen saw the problem
And with just a word or two
Offered then and there to fix
The issue we all knew.

I'd tried a frontal fastening
The hooks were way too small.
My aging fingers could not cope
With tiny hooks at all.

I've tried the bras that have no hooks.
You climb in, if you can
But that was just as hard for me.
I'm not happy Jan.

I know my breasts are floppy
So I really need support.
I'm not sure of the solution.
Going braless, that's a rort.

So just for now the answer
Is dear Colleen's helping hand,
Which fixes hooks to trap my boobs,
I think she's really grand.

I can manage of a morning
When I'm getting dressed alone
But when I've aqua exercised
My arms just feel like stone.

So, thank you dearest Colleen
Who closes hooks each time
Encasing saggy bosoms.
You really are sublime.

I picture you in heaven
With all the angel host
Doing up their bras all day
Where they'll reward you most!

Times have changed

Written to acknowledge Stephen Taberner and the Spooky Men's chorale, who provided virtual entertainment during lock down.

We're all in isolation
Of one sort or another;
If it wasn't for Covid 19,
We wouldn't have to bother.

It's doing what all viruses do
But causing much more trouble,
That's why all we Aussies
Must stay inside our bubble.

Keep your distance all the time
Wash your hands and sanitise,
We have to beat this virus;
Don't be foolish, please be wise.

Essential workers, thank you,
For keeping up the fight,
Kids, enjoy home schooling,
Make sure you get it right!

Thank you Stephen and your busy crew
For setting up the virtual choir,
And giving us a challenge
When things around are dire.

Music is the food of love,
It's perfect for our soul,
It cheers us up when we are down
And makes sure we stay whole.

So raise your voices once again,
Make the music swell;
When we come out the other side
We pray all will be well.

7 April 2020

Photo courtesy of Minh Hien and Farshid

In Self-Isolation

Oh how I miss my aqua class
While in self-isolation.
I've rung some friends to have a chat
And all feel the devastation.

Much as we loved our exercise
And all the lovely trainers
Chatting to our aqua friends
Is one of life's no brainers.

Social aspects of our class
It's absolutely clear
Are so important for us all
And things we all hold dear.

We're chatting on the telephone
And checking on our friends
These things will keep our peckers up
And pay out dividends.

What substitutes have you found out there?
What exercises can you do?
Have you found that climbing up the wall
Relieves a pain or two?

I walk the dogs each morning
But then I always did;
Find me an impactless substitute
Before I lift the lid.

There's nothing like the pool we know,
And splashing in the water.
We truly love the exercise
And know we really oughter.

There is a great temptation
When staying home alone,
To nibble on those little treats
Within the pantry zone.

Extra cuppas now and then
And the occasional biscuit
Without our exercise at all
We really shouldn't risk it.

I can feel the waistband shrinking
Or is it me that's growing?
If this goes on much longer,
Tummies will be overflowing.

Can you imagine how it will be
When on the other side,
We return to Aqua twice as fat
Because exercise was denied?

We're thinking of our trainers
And all the lovely staff
Who keep the centre going;
It's certainly no laugh.

Times are tough for many
We feel their pain and worry,
And wish them peace of mind and hope
That Covid 19's end will hurry.

Remember that we value you
And one day we'll get together.
We pray the darkest clouds will lift
And we'll be back to sunny weather.

March 2020

The Aqua Video

Guess what! We're going to be film stars;
Who would ever think?
Bec and friends will film us;
We're theatrically on the brink!

She thinks we all have talent,
I wonder if she's right;
We'll find out soon, that is for sure
When we watch the film one night.

Our aqua group is special
We've known for many years;
This group, which tries to care for all.
Through laughter and through tears.

When times are good we laugh a lot,
When things are hard, we cry;
Our aqua group shows its concern
And helps us all get by.

It now will be on record,
This kind, supportive group
Will turn up trumps on video,
And we'll all be in the loop.

Bec and Ninna and their friends
Are going to try to capture
The essence of our aqua group,
The delight, the fun and rapture!

We may be getting older,
Not exactly bathing belles;
But that won't be the story
That this video truly tells!

It will tell the world that aqua
Is great for one and all.
That in a class like our class,
Everyone can have a ball!

August 2020

Mid-Year Christmas 2022

I miss deep water aqua,
The physio says "Too cold,"
Instead, I potter in warm water,
Doing as I'm told.

Does this let me off the hook
In terms of writing rhyme?
No, money raising for MND means
I must write rhymes all the time!

And you, my caring aqua friends
Help me raise the cash
With your donations when we meet
At our mid-year Christmas bash.

I'm grateful that you're generous;
We'll beat this dreaded curse,
One day there'll be no MND
(And I won't be writing verse!)

Thanks to Stan for his hard work.
And thanks to Lizzie too
For getting us all together,
That's you and you and you!

I hope you choose a scrumptious meal;
Do have a joyful time.
It's Christmas time in winter
And the company's sublime!

At the aquatic centre
Things are changing slowly.
Women are using urinals?
Goodness, holy moley.

We'll get our change room back one day;
The blokes will get theirs too.
We wish lockers opened every time.
Which is what they're meant to do!

Enjoy your aqua at the pool;
Do as the trainers say,
And you could be fit and healthy
For ever and a day

Maintaining fitness is such fun
And the friendships are a joy.
Come on, get your bathers on.
No need to be coy!

For those who could not make it here,
Be sure you're not forgotten.
We're missing you and thinking that
Your absence is just rotten.

Happy mid-year Christmas
To everyone who's here.
Thank you all for coming.
We'll be back again next year.

June 2022

No distance of place or lapse of time
can lessen the friendship of those
who are thoroughly persuaded of each other's worth.

Robert Southey

There are many farewells at aqua.

We have lost some dear friends and others have moved away.

One of our class, Donna, became a trainer and then went into real estate. She has made other moves subsequently.

Vivien was a real live wire at aqua and a good friend. We were not pleased when she decided to return to Perth, but could not blame her for wanting to be nearer family.

Vale Simon was for the conductor of the Tasmanian University Music Society with whom I sang for several years.

I had previously sung with Sisonke and later with the Tasmanian Chorale. Singing has been another of the great delights of my life.

Donna's departure

I'm heading off to Canberra,
My daughter's had an op.
Sorry I can't be at your "do"
Regret I cannot stop.

When first we knew you Donna,
You were in our aqua class.
You joined in all the aqua moves
And stretched from head to ... toe!

And then you did a training course.
It changed your role forever.
Instructor, leader, trainer, you
Are really very clever.

We've watched you grow in confidence
You've moved from shy and quiet
To confident, near extrovert.
Your classes are a riot!

We've followed you in every sense;
We've loved our contact with you;
Your empathy and quiet wit,
Your caring nature too.

We do not really understand
How you could leave us, truly.
We half expect to see you back
Before we turn unruly.

What do you see in real estate?
And Pam Corkhill as your boss;
Does she know she has a gem
And we a mighty loss?

We're here to say our au revoirs,
To thank and wish you well.
You will charm realtor types
And make the houses sell!

Dear Donna please do not forget
Your erstwhile aqua friends,
For we shall all remember you
While doing aqua bends!

2009

Memory Necklace

Dear Vivien, as you leave us
I've made this gift for you
To say how much I'll miss you.
Maybe you'll miss me too!

If you look carefully at the beads
You'll see few are the same;
Each represents a memory;
You can give each bead a name.

There are two fish you'll notice;
They represent our swims.
The butterfly's for happiness,
Before the memory dims.

Each bead is someone different;
You can choose who's what.
The main thing is your aqua friends
Do not wish to be forgot!

Choose a bead for Helen
For she will miss you badly;
You've been a special friend for her;
She will be lonely, sadly.

The filler beads are golden orbs;
I know you like things shiny;
They represent our lovely chats-
Some long and others tiny!

Don't forget the trainers
Who supervise the pool.
They train us up so very well,
And fitness is their rule.

The refugees would send their love,
If they knew that you were going;
You've boosted up their wardrobes
And saved a lot of sewing!

I have benefitted too,
My wardrobe's been extended;
Colours that I've never worn
Which surprisingly have blended!

This necklace then is a small gift
To say how much I'll miss you.
Thank you for just who you are
And know that God will bless you.

From Margaret with love,
October 2021.

Vale Simon

Dear Simon, as you leave us,
We wish you all the best,
We thank you for the music,
The singing and the rest.

For TUMS must do without you.
We'll miss you and your ways.
We'll focus on the memories
Of all those halcyon days.

We know that your composing
Has flourished and has grown,
And when you have your tantrums,
You can have them on your own!

We'll see your name in writing,
Reviews, we have no doubt
Will praise your latest efforts.
And give your work some clout.

Come Christmas at the Royal
We hope you'll sing along.
The carols and reunion
Are special times of song.

We wonder of you'll miss us,
The TUMS celestial choir;
Now others will inspire us
And light our music fire.

Don't worry. We will manage,
We'll never give up singing.
Whatever happens TUMS remains
And joyous sounds keeps bringing.

So leave us now, go safely,
Compose to heart's content.
Contact your groups and teach the kids,
There's nothing to lament!

Cherish all your happy moments;
they make a fine cushion for old age.

Booth Tarkington

There are many jingles for birthday celebrations. The first in this collection is to celebrate my son's 40th birthday. Chris would not be alive if it were not for Dr Gabriel Zatlin who saved his life in Indonesia when he contracted meningococcal disease. We sent a jingle for his 60th birthday. Two jingles are for my step-grandchildren. Many jingles are for Stan. Stan gets most of the birthday jingles as he has long celebrated his birthdays with his aqua friends and he just keeps on having birthdays!

Photo courtesy of Minh Hien and Farshid

Chris turns 40 and we celebrate in Brisbane. August 2009

Our Chris is turning forty;
Oh, what a joyous day
Reminding us of pleasures
And thrills along the way.

He's had his special moments,
Some good and others bad,
But through it all we love him,
He's such a gorgeous lad!

When Chris was just an infant
He had sisters two above,
Surrounded by his family
He had unconditional love.

He was a ray of sunshine,
A bouncy, bonny boy.
His blue eyes and his blonde hair
Filled everyone with joy.

And then a baby brother,
One Timothy by name,
Became his younger sibling.
We were so glad that he came.

Chris was a caring brother,
He loved the little one
And shared his toys and playthings,
Until the day was done.

When Chris became a schoolboy
His teachers loved him too
And all the little schoolgirls
Did what most school girls do!

He came and told his Mummy
"I hate those kissing girls,
They chase me round the playground
And mess up all my curls".

In Java, Indonesia
We went to meet his Dad
But Chris complained of headaches
And said his neck was bad.

The doctors said "It's dengue"
They really didn't know.
Thank God for Dr Zatlin.
It was meningitis, so!

Chris was an avid sportsman,
First soccer was his game,
Then badminton and cricket
But each of these proved tame.....

.... until he took up rugby.
That really was his sport.
There he found his forte
And played it like he ought!

He travelled once to Fiji,
To play with Uni Sevens;
A competition glorious;
He thought he was in heaven.

Until a bit of coral
Cut him on the foot.
He ended up in hospital,
He nearly was kaput!

The world is now his oyster,
He's travelled far and wide,
And has wife, Ann, his soulmate
To travel by his side.

He has three gorgeous children
Ella, Jack and Finn.
His business is 4Impact.
He cannot fail to win!

We wish him Happy Birthday
Two score years and then.
All the best and lots of love.
Best Wishes, once again.

In nineteen seventy-five
Chris was more dead than alive.
At Indon's Pertamina,
Doc Z was much keener
To heal him and help him survive.

Chris Eldridge continued to thrive
And reunions have numbered five.
Phil, Sally and Kathryn
Met Dr Gabriel Zatlin
Then Marg flew and Chris made the drive.

Happy Birthday Gabriel, friend,
You fixed Chris and helped him to mend.
You're loved and admired
And we are inspired.
We'll be friends right on to the end!

To Lorna and Sarah we send
Our greetings so hastily penned.
We wish we could be there,
And if there were free fare
We'd arrive instead of pretend!

For My Step-grandchildren

Two birthday jingles follow; written for my step-grandchildreen. They have been very accommodating about acquiring another grandmother. As if two were not enough! Their birthdays are on three consecutive days.

Tom, here's your Birthday lemon curd

To share with Ben and Sarah.

They have the bread and butter spread,

So nothing could be fairer!

A loaf of bread for you dear Ben;

The butter is with Sarah,

And Tom has lemon curd to share;

He's been chosen as the carer!

This butter is your birthday gift;

The bread's with Ben your brother

And you all have home-made lemon curd

To share with one another!

Photo courtesy of Ellyse Tran and Tri Tri Tran,
from Ellyse (aged 16)'s watercolour painting.

Too Many Birthdays!

This year's birthday gifts were hidden in the wrong bedrooms.

I think I may have got mixed up,
And gifts have gone awry.
What did I plan for Sarah?
If she wants it she must try!

And Ben, I really cannot think,
My mind is growing dim,
So if he wants his present
It's really up to him!

Now Tom's another problem,
What did I choose for him?
His chances now of finding it
Are really looking slim!

So to the darling trio:
I hope you'll sort it out,
And Happy Birthday each of you
You're fabulous, no doubt.

With love from Nanna Margaret, June 2015.

Photo courtesy of Minh Hien and Farshid

Stan's Birthday Jingle

Our Stan's achieved another year
And hence this celebration
With friends-his aquarobics mates,
Such joy and jubilation!

What can we say about our Stan?
He's been around for ages,
And those who've aquarobed with him
Have shared in many stages!

He's made us laugh. He's made us cry,
We've grieved with him for Shirley
And Scot his very special son,
And lots more hurley burley.

Our friend Stan's boys- dear Mat and Ned
Provide so much delight;
There's humour there and lots of fun
From serious to trite!

The Tuesday breakfasts are renowned,
The neighbourhood appears
And breakfast goes right on til lunch
As it has done for some for years!

Stan drives his faithful BM Dub,
He's always there as friend;
Lifts and chores and visits too
And humour without end!

His faithful walker keeps him up
Instead of tipping over;
And now the hoist beside the pool
Ensures that he's in clover!

So Happy Birthday dearest Stan,
You are a national treasure;
Enjoy your day and all it brings;
Good wishes beyond measure!

September 2016

Not another Birthdy Stan. Pressure is mounting!!!

The "Patriarch of Aqua" you,
The one we all adore.
But Stan, it's getting difficult
To dream up any more.

I've really run out of ideas,
There've been so many years,
I've written birthday lines for you;
You'll soon have me in tears!

I've talked about our name for you,
It's Stan the Man of course.
You've earned it 'cos you swim with girls,
And demonstrate such force.

I've talked about your woodwork skills
And all the things you fix;
And how your generosity
Provides a lovely mix.

I've written words that sing your praise
Extolled the man you are.
I've even said your character
Has made you quite a star.

I've talked about your family too
And just how grand they are.
And how they mean so much to you,
And I'll not forget that car!

Now have I mentioned those two cats
That race along your hall?
And how they really rule the roost
With seven legs in all.

I've said that we all love you Stan,
And all of us agree,
The aqua class would be quite dull
If you weren't there you see.

I've talked about the jokes you tell
And how you reminisce.
I've even praised your friendliness
And now it's come to this.

I haven't any other things
That I can think to say
Except to wish you from us all
A Very Happy Day.

Sept 10th 2014

Stan's 80ᵗʰ Birthday

Last year Liz baked a birthday cake;
It was Stan's special 80.
How wrong we were, out by one year,
(We were trying to be matey).

This time we know we've got it right;
Goodbye to seventy-nine
And welcome to another year,
We want it to be fine.

For "Stan the man", he is our friend;
What would we do without him?
He cheers us up and takes such care,
He has an air about him.

Stan aquaed first in Dockside days.
Down to the wharf he sprinted,
And when they closed that swimming pool,
His Tatts aqua card was printed.

We met him first at aqua class,
The brave bloke with the women.
He doesn't seem to mind at all
That with females he is swimmin'.

In fact I think we make his day,
We ladies are his treasure.
We brighten up his dullest times
And give dear Stan much pleasure.

We may not all be bathing belles
But what we lack in beauty,
Imagination, and Stan has lots,
Ensures he does his duty.

Of course there are some other blokes
Who join us in the water,
But Stan's been round twenty-plus years;
(I think he knows he oughter!)

He greets us all with cheery words,
Our dumb-bells he arranges
And puts our belts out on the chairs
And notices the changes.

Stan tells us all his family news,
Of Shirley, Matt and Scott
And Ned the grandson he adores.
He loves the whole darned lot.

He's special carer to his Shirl
He tends her with such ardour.
She and the boys enjoy the meals
Created from his larder.

He is a chef of some repute;
We love his contributions
To morning tea and aqua lunch.
He offers great solutions.

There's quiches baked with pastry crisp
And sandwiches, the club sort,
And wondrous egg and bacon pies.
Stan never sells us short.

We haven't had a curry yet,
Though from India he came;
Maybe the chilli is too hot,
And none of us is game.

Though born of English heritage,
Stan barracks for Australia;
He's lived all over Hobart town
With all his paraphernalia.

Stan's business skills and trading nouse
Have served him well I'll wager.
He knows just everyone in town
He doesn't need a pager.

Stan fixes things for many folk;
He fixed my little table.
So "Goodman" is appropriate,
His goodness is no fable!

While we are special to our Stan,
He is our aqua hero.
Congratulations Stan, you've added to the 8
a special, momentous, wonderful, earth-
shaking, pivotal, significant, remarkable,
life-changing zero.
.

Sept 8th 2010

Jingles and Me by Margaret Eldridge AM

Happy Birthday Stan, 2018

I didn't think you'd need me
To write a birthday jingle,
Although this group of aqua friends
Has gathered here to mingle.

I wasn't going to write you know,
But last night I couldn't sleep
Until I scribbled down my thoughts;
This jingle wouldn't keep.

2.30 in the morning
I found myself awake
And jotted down this little rhyme,
All for our dear Stan's sake.

It isn't that I'm lazy,
Just that sometimes I get tired,
But I had to write this jingle down,
For that's the way I'm wired!

Happy Birthday Stanley,
Enjoy your birthday lunch
Along with all your aqua mates,
A very friendly bunch.

We wish you every happiness
For ever and a day
And hope these little gifts
Will keep you clean along the way.

We know Imperial Leather
Is your very favourite soap
So cleanliness and godliness is
Our very fervent hope!

We love you our dear Stanley John
Really such a Goodman(!),
Enjoy this latest birthday
In any way you can!

Raise your glasses one and all
A toast for 87,
And may this great occasion
Bring you a touch of heaven!

Sept 2018

For Stan, Celebrating 90, Sep 8th 2021

(To be sung to Click go the Shears.)

1 Now that he's 90 our dear friend Stan
Stands here before us a generous man,
He's friend to us all, a very kind chap
Happily, we greet him for his 91st lap!
Chorus Let's raise a toast to our dear friend Stan;
We lovingly call him "Stan the Man";
Goodman by name and by nature too,
He's the sort of bloke that everyone turns to.

2 When you need a lift 'cos you haven't got your car,
Stan the Man will drive you anywhere, near or far.
If you've forgotten money for your drink,
Stan will sub you willingly. Quicker than you think!

3 Aqua's his scene, this is where he's at,
(Can you see he's lost 10 kgs of fat?)
He chats to us all as he swims around the pool;
We're not supposed to chatter, but Stan breaks the rule! **Chorus**

4 We're friends and fellow travellers, aqua is so good,
If you haven't tried it yet, we think you really should.
We're very companionable, we saved Stan's life,
Looking out for anyone in any kind of strife.

5 Stan is a film star of international fame.
Our aqua class was filmed and here is the name,
"An Aquatic Community" is an absolute joy
Rudolph Valentino, shove over, Stan's the new boy! **Chorus**

6 Stan's friends are many and lots of them are here
And as for all his rellies, he really holds them dear.
Let's raise a glass and wish him all the best,
After all the jollity he might need a Granfer rest.

7 Here's to you dear Stan, our 90 yr old friend,
And many birthday wishes we happily send.
We wish you all the best and many birthdays more;
We'll celebrate again when 100 is the score! **Chorus.**

Yulia's Big Eight-O

Our Birthday Girl is glamourous,
She's a very striking blonde.
We met her first through aqua
And quickly struck a bond.

Her swimming costumes are a dream;
They come from overseas.
They make the rest of us look plain;
(And check out her new knees!)

She left her native Hungary
In circumstances rotten;
That part of her history
Is probably best forgotten.

She made a very perilous trek
To escape a dreadful fate.
She lived with other refugees,
Trying not to hate.

But Yulia's a survivor;
She built a brand new life
In her new home, Australia
Away from Europe's strife.

She put in a lot of effort
Creating family for sure;
Raised two special children
And asked for little more.

She dressed our lady Lord Mayor
Doone Kennedy by name:
Yulia stitched and tailored;
No two outfits were the same.

Our swimming pool acknowledges
Doone's efforts with much pride,
While Yulia splashes round with us
Exercising far and wide.

And then life took a u-turn;
Yulia studied art
And focused on ceramics
Which played the major part.

Her crystalline creations
And Southern Ice latticed pieces
Are testament to wondrous skill
Which never ever ceases.

She moulds and sculpts each special piece,
The kiln must then be lit
And out come lovely objects
Bit by precious bit.

Yulia now has fame achieved,
Her creativity's well known
And her beautiful ceramics
At Salamanca now are shown.

Yulia's had some struggles
And so have some of us,
 But counselling for Life –line
Was certainly a plus.

Yulia is a singer too
She sings along with Nourish
A choir which gives much pleasure
So long may Nourish flourish.

Yulia has an idol,
A conductor of great fame;
I don't really need to tell you
André Rieu is his name!

Yulia's garden is a true delight
It always looks so neat
And as we celebrate her birthday
We are all in for a treat.

Her Hungarian cakes are legendry,
She makes them every year
To celebrate at Christmas
And fill us with good cheer.

Friendship's high on Yulia's list,
She cherishes us all,
So here's to her, the birthday girl
Yulia's 80! Have a ball!
Happy Birthday Yulia!

January 2018

On my celebrating 80

I celebrated 80 with a wonderful party lunch at the Fern Tree Community Hall.
85 will be quieter!

> I always write a ditty
> I know it is expected.
> So, cheer up folks, put on a grin
> And do not look dejected.
>
> Eighty years and going strong
> Despite a few hard knocks.
> You cannot reach the summit
> Without climbing over rocks!
>
> The pleasures truly far outweigh,
> I'm grateful for my friends
> And if I have offended you
> I hope to make amends!
>
> I've drawn you altogether;
> My friends are by my side,
> So thank you all for coming
> And joining in my ride,
>
> It's been a wondrous journey,
> You've helped to shape the way
> By offering me your friendship
> For ever and a day.
>
> We never know our future,
> What things will come along;
> But if life is a melody,
> I'll greet it with a song!!!

Siebrand's Celebration

Here's to Siebrand, faithful friend
Who's reached the allotted span,
The biblical three score years and ten,
Outdo it if you can!

Our friendship goes back many years,
Church music was our aim,
With Carol's lead, Consort was formed
And various singers came.

We livened up the services
With Bach, Purcell and Parry.
We filled the church with glorious works
To inspire Tom, Dick and Harry.

Siebrand plays the organ too-
He may not be a master.
But we delight in what he does,
There's rarely a disaster!

Siebrand came from Holland's shore
To Penguin with his kin,
And then to PNG he went,
Took Carol for a spin.

When they returned with children six
And wondrous tales to tell,
They ended up at Hobart's Tab,
We got to know them well.

A time there was in New South Wales
For Bible Society work.
They travelled all round the world
For Siebrand could not shirk!

The children did as scripture bids,
Went forth and multiplied.
They're spread around the continent.
In them Siebrand takes pride!

The grandchildren are numerous
And married now are some.
Siebrand, beloved progenitor
Has great-grandchildren yet to come!

Despite some major surgery
Siebrand's still hale and hearty.
He bears his years extremely well.
He's ready now to party!

His biography's done for all to read,
He's set it out in detail,
A life of rich experiences,
Including some in retail.

So happy birthday Siebrand dear,
(Your moustache is quite a feature!)
Enjoy yourself, have lots of fun,
Signed: Margaret Eldridge, Teacher!!!

Siebrand turns 80

Our Siebrand's turning eighty,
A most impressive score,
We wish him a happy birthday
And many, many more.

I want to tell his story
As briefly as I can,
But that may be a problem,
He's been a very busy man!

The start of course was Holland,
In Haren I've been told;
He followed on five others
In the Petrusma fold.

His country suffered in the war,
And then a big decision
To head off to Australia
And fulfil a larger vision.

They settled in Tasmania,
In Penguin of all places;
At school he learned the lingo
And was soon put through his paces.

Work started as an office boy,
And then the Burnie Mill,
And then a hospital visit
Provided Siebrand with a thrill.

He met again his future wife,
Nurse Carol Boyes by name.
In no time Siebrand had proposed
Hereon, the marriage game.

A teaching job in PNG,
Rabaul and then with Agarabi,
Ann and Vicki soon arrived
(Find a word to rhyme wit Agarabi!)

Now add Mark and Brenda,
And then came twins once more;
Tim and Heather joined the clan
Making Six the final score.

We meet them next in Hobart,
When it became their base
And Siebrand worked at projects
All around the place.

With Guide Dogs for the Blind I think
He really made his mark,
His business enterprise was clear,
Can you hear the Guide Dogs bark?

A stint away in Sydney,
We missed our special friends,
But back they came to join us all
And start some different trends.

And then his darling Carol,
Such a talented musician,
Got sick and sadly passed away;
His life was in transition.

Siebrand's heart was broken,
We watched and grieved with him,
"Where to now?" he questioned
And life alone was grim.

Then he told me of a visit
To Sydney friends for dinner,
They'd lined up several ladies,
And one, she was a winner.

We joined in his excitement,
We welcomed his new wife.
Jan's the best thing to have happened,
In this newest phase in life.

She's taken on the challenge
Of a family rather large
With descendants by the dozen,
And Siebrand there in charge!

Children and grandchildren,
And another generation,
And more to come I'd say,
In fact a delegation!

He's faced some stressful issues,
He's had some major ops,
But surgeons here in Hobart,
They really are the tops.

He's done a lot more travelling
To countries far and wide;
Back to his precious PNG
With dear Jan at his side.

Siebrand, thank you for the friendship
You've shown to all of us,
Knowing you is special
And certainly a plus.

Thanks for all the music,
The organ and the singing,
The moustachios and lovely smile.
And voice so deep and ringing.

Happy birthday Siebrand,
How fortunate you've been,
Thank God for all the wondrous years
And all the things you've seen.

With blessings more to follow,
We wish you all the best
For today's great celebration
And of course, for all the rest.

April 2019

Jingles and Me by Margaret Eldridge AM

Martin's Milestone

Here's to Martin, faithful friend
Who's reached the allotted span-
The biblical three score years and ten.
Outdo it if you can.

Our friendship covers many years
But before we ever met
We child-hooded in Babbacombe;
The evacuated wartime set.

Our dads were handsome sailors
Who served the navy well
On board the Royal Sovereign
With wartime tales to tell.

And then the lovely Myrna,
My bridesmaid true was she,
In Miri, Shell employed them both;
She told me where he'd be.

So when my dentist proved so rude
I searched for Martin B
To take his place and do my teeth,
Repairs you cannot see!

Fillings, caps and X-rays too,
Gold crowns and much, much more;
Injections strong to hide the pain
I felt on Kingston's shore.

His tender touch and music sweet
With paintings on the wall,
Made the experience almost fun;
His charm delighted all.

Patricia fell for all his ways,
And yes, I knew her too.
Another life consumed us both,
But Martin wooed her true.

And now retirement's claimed him,
To Yellow Point I'll go
To chat about the good old days
And people that we know.

Happy Birthday Martin dear
With bells and knobs on too.
Enjoy your life, have lots of fun-
My birthday wish for you!

Maureen's Moments

The invite said 'No fuss, no mess,
No clearing up, no cooking!'
So I replied "I'd love to come",
And Maureen made the booking.

Maureen says she's turning sixty;
Hard to believe that's true.
The years have been most kind to her;
You wouldn't have a clue!

Maureen's skills as a teacher,
Devoted to education,
Have spread her influence far and wide,
Right across the nation!

And further still, around the world
Her legendry travelling's famous.
She's covered ground much more than most,
Adventurous trips to shame us.

One thing you cannot fail to note,
The purple influence on her.
From head to toe, quite literally,
She pays the colour honour!

So here's to Maureen's sixtieth,
Years worth celebrating.
Your friends admire your attitude
Of glass half full and waiting!

For Andrea at Her Half Century

I said "I won't write a jingle
Or an inappropriate song",
But on most special occasions,
One seems to come along!

Tim's our son, a handsome lad,
We've watched him grow with pride.
And looked on with approval
When he took Andrea as his bride.

Andrea is a lawyer
With a very able mind,
She excels in more directions;
She really was a find!

Her cooking is superlative,
Her cup cakes are divine,
I really cannot fault one bit
This daughter-in-law of mine.

She's capable, a manager,
She's doing further study.
I admire her distinctive dress sense,
She's not a fuddy-duddy.

Her shoes are quite remarkable,
She wears them with a flare;
Move over Imelda Marcos,
Ignore her if you dare!

Caitlin makes up the trio
And brings us all much joy.
What would they have called her
If she had been a boy?

Their home is up the mountain;
And sometimes they get snow.
It's visited by wildlife
And a lovely place to go.

Some creatures visit often,
Such a treat to see,
Paddymelons, potoroos and bird-life,
As happy as can be.

The resident two rabbits
Are not allowed to roam.
But with rose petals and cuddles
They have the perfect home.

And now this celebration,
Fifty years for sure,
My loved and loving daughter-in-law,
I wish you many more.

With candles and a birthday cake
And friends and family too,
A golden chance to sing out loud,
Happy Birthday to You.

September 2021

Extract from Dame Edna Everage's thoughts on marriage

I was asked to say a few words about marriage at a party . I refused saying since I was a divorcee, I wasn't the best person to ask. I had second thoughts and offered to take on the persona of Dame Edna Everage, famed Australian comedian and pass some of her recorded comments about her own marriage to Norm of Moonee Ponds, Melbourne and her family of four. I dressed in full Dame Edna regalia, including a bunch of her trademark gladdies which I tossed around the room. One little boy asked his mother "Is she the queen?" I have edited this jingle a little for inclusion in this book.

Junette, party organiser supreme, planned a party for a number of church folk who were celebrating their 70th birthdays but I was unable to attend so, guess what, I sent a jingle. Another memorable party was when we celebrated Max and Junette's Golden Wedding (a year late because Junette was in hospital on the official date!)

I'm sure you all know who I am,
Dame Edna, super-star.
I gather nuptials are planned,
So possums, here we are.

But first some words about moi,
I do not wish to brag
Of marriage, but I know a lot
My own? Out of the bag!

Dear Norm, my late lamented,
Died after prostate troubles,
But when I reached his death-bed,
All that was left was bubbles!

Just a dent upon his pillow,
Globally recycled he had been,
The cremation was a waste of cash,
No ashes to be seen!

My mother, well she's half alive
Incarcerated true,
The Twilight Home for the Bewildered,
Just to give a clue.

Now Kenny, Bruce and Valmai,
My offspring minus one,
They do me proud most of the time,
But Lois was abducted and then became a nun!

It's not that I don't like Catholics,
Though a Protestant I am.
She's missed out on a wedding
And pushing round a pram.

Childbirth four times over
(We couldn't take the pill)
Norm and I, our private life
Was sometimes overkill!

A couple hoping to conceive
Asked me for advice.
I told them "Try the usual way"
(Norm reckoned it was nice.)

My Kenny's a dress designer
(He's designing all the time!)
His "partner" Cliff can't find Miss Right
Nor Kenny (past his prime!)

My Brucie married Joylene,
Such a gorgeous pair.
Dear Norm would be so very proud
If he's looking down up there.

Valmai, well what can I say?
She tries to do her best,
But dealing with my new cosmetic range
Has put her to the test.

Melbourne loves me this I know,
With statue, street name, stamp.
The problem though with Moonee Ponds,
Is, it's often very damp.

My wall to wall burgundy carpet
Is such tasteful decoration.
It's been copied all around the town
Flattery by imitation.

Jingles and Me by Margaret Eldridge AM

Nancy Reagan's astrologer
(I knew dear Nancy well)
Said I was Scarlet O'Hara
In a former life she'd tell.

I'll introduce you both to my son Ken,
He'll dress you for the day;
A tux and gown to suit you both;
(Of course, you'll have to pay.)

Dear Madge Allsop was my bridesmaid,
She did the job quite well,
But as she's six feet under,
We'll find another girl.

I'm sure you'll carry flowers
On your wedding day;
I think they should be gladdies
To send you on your way.

I could give you lots more good advice
But in a private session.
Just let me know when's best for you.
And I'll fit in that progression.

Best wishes for your marriage;
I'm sure you've chosen well.
With wedding etiquette in hand
I've no doubt that you'll gel.

Photo courtesy of Ellyse Tran and Tri Tri Tran, from Ellyse (aged 11)'s watercolour painting.

The Birthday Concert

I've heard about the birthdays;
My goodness what a lot!
If I remember rightly
It's seventy years you've got.

I'm sure that you all realise
That three score years and ten
Is our allotted span here,
For women and for men.

I'm sorry I can't be there
To join in all the fun;
I'm at a conference in Adelaide;
I'll come home when it is done.

You know I wrote my thesis,
The story of the Hmong.
I shared it at this conference.
My presentation wasn't long.

I love to meet the others;
They're history buffs like me.
We're into oral history
Telling stories as you see.

I wonder if your stories
Of the seventy years you've had
Are written down, recorded,
Were you good or were you bad?

Did you view the Ten Commandments
As a guide, or did you break
A number of them badly?
Are you a roué or a rake?

I'm sure you've been exemplary,
You've lived your lives full well
As no doubt these celebrations
Will surely show and tell!

My greetings come across the miles,
Happy Birthday to you all.
Enjoy the celebrations,
Make sure you have a ball.

Kick up your heels, get lively,
Just show them what you've got!
You really have a duty
To give it your best shot!

And when I'm back in Hobart
I'll want to see you all
On video and camera
As you frolicked in the hall!

I'm sure the decorations
Will be up there with the best
With Junette there supervising
They will have had to pass the test!

The items for the concert,
I can just imagine those,
With lots of fun and laughter
At the music and the prose.

So rock on all you trendies,
Show the youngsters how it is,
We oldies still have quality
And huge amounts of fizz!

With love, Margaret (aged almost 76)

For Max and Junette

How dare I write a jingle
For the jingle-writing queen?
And for her consort Maxie;
By her side he's always been.

Well, here is my confession,
Junette asked me to you see,
So I could say the things she can't,
Whatever they may be.

So first, re Max's birthday,
Eighty, what a score,
Happy Birthday wishes,
And hopes for many more!

And then the fifty years plus one,
(The golden year passed by).
Dear Junette wasn't very well,
But this year she's more spry.

Congratulations of the golden sort
We much admire your grit,
To stick it out for all that time-
Must've been the perfect fit!

And now some family details
You may already know;
Parents of two lovely kids
Who now it's time to show.

Russel, he's the loving son,
Please stand up for us now,
And Cheralynne, please, on your feet
And take a timely bow!

Another generation now,
Is growing up for sure
They're apples in the loving eyes
Of grandparents and more.

At what do these three kids excel?
Two were on stage in Mary Poppins
And whatever else you say of them,
They certainly weren't just drop-ins!

Tom the third declined this time,
He's died three times on stage.
He wants to be a stay-at-home mum.
He's a laugh on every page!

On your feet Amelia, Sam and Tom,
Give us all a look,
Honour your loving grandparents
As explained in the Good Book!

And others are related,
Family far and wide,
Please stand with Max and Junette
No matter from which side.

So that leaves all the rest of us;
We are just their friends
Who've come along to sing and dance,
Do knees up and the bends.

For Junette loves a party,
She's organised a few,
So crazy larks are nothing
When you are with these two.

I don't know where she finds the games
Clever competitions and quizzes,
You can be sure she'll dream some up
Before this party fizzes!

Throughout the years here at the Tab
Junette's had this hall humming,
And Max has put up with it all
Including guitars, choirs and drumming.

The Pope was here and good Queen Liz
And even Dame Edna Everage.
She threw her gladdies all around
Whatever was her beverage?

Baby showers and birthdays,
Women's stuff and singing;
Engagements, weddings and much more
Have set these arches ringing!

So if you aren't the party type,
Now's the time to leave,
Before the fun and nonsense starts,
There will be no reprieve!

I can't forget to mention
Meet and Make for sure,
This lovely couple organised
For eleven years and more.

Each Friday during term time
They got the old hall ready
For groups of more mature folk,
Most of whom were steady!

Activities abounded,
And friendships, how they grew,
And Max and Junette dreamt up stuff
And knew just what to do.

Lots of fun and laughter too;
Participants were clever,
And people came from far and wide
So they could be togever.

Max took charge of outings
A couple times a year
And though we paid for tickets
They really were not dear.

I remember when Graham Clements
Extolled about the trains
As we travelled to the Midlands
And then back home again.

South Arm and the Huon
Gardens really beaut,
Coaches mostly comfortable;
It was Max worked out the route.

There are some stories I could tell
But I'll leave them for Junette.
She'll write another jingle,
She won't let you forget!

So here's to this lovely couple
With numerous good wishes
For all the gifts they've shared with us.
Please stay on and wash the dishes!

April 2018

The Lady Nelson

My friend Gary Easthope is a volunteer looking after *The Lady Nelson*. It is a replica of the original vessel and takes tourist down the river. Gary asked if I could write a jingle for the crew. He planned to use it to raise funds to assist with the costs associated with the vessel. He gave me an article he had written about the Lady Nelson and I used that as a basis for the jingle.

I tell the tale of a small, brave brig,
Lady Nelson is her name;
She's a replica of an historic boat,
A ship of no small fame!

Tasmanians love their heritage
And despite the enormous cost,
The Friends of the Lady Nelson
Were determined she'd not be lost!

They fought the Government and more;
They planned to bring her back.
She would not stay in Hastings, Vic.,
But take another tack.

When your ship's a special icon
You cannot let her go;
You battle the detractors
And tell them clearly "No!"

Aboard a former ferry
Moored in Hobart Town
The Friends of the Lady Nelson
Beat the opposition down.

They chose a crew of sailors
Who left to start their task,
But when they reached where she was moored
They clearly had to ask.......

"What have you done to our brave ship?
Why the disarray?
Why no maintenance to date?
On her we cannot stay.

With maggots in the freezer
And carpets clearly rotten
And mildew in the bulkheads
How could you have forgotten?"

Despite the mess, the flag went up,
Hoisted on the mast;
Three hearty cheers from all aboard
And cleaning up was fast.

The ratlines they were rotten,
Rigging, some was missing;
Shackles and chain were tightened up
Amidst cursing and some hissing!

The motor needed fixing,
Electricians got it going;
Batteries were all replaced,
There was no need for towing.

The bills at the marina
Were paid but minus some,
For clearly cleaning wasn't done;
Then fuel bills to come.

The Lady Nelson sailed again
Across our wild Bass Strait.
The anchor, it was nearly lost;
There was an anxious wait.

From Ball Bay, Bruny Island,
The Lady Nelson sailed
Back to her home port, Hobart;
The crew had never failed!

The welcome was tremendous;
The Friends and many more
Were at the docks in Hobart
As the crew all came ashore.

The story doesn't end here;
The debt was huge you know,
But trips, weddings and lots else
Have helped the coffers grow.

Maintenance and training,
A new galley, cabin roof,
Fuel and water tanks replaced,
As if you needed proof.

The engine took a beating;
Reconditioning was advised
And rot was found along a rail;
Repairs were then devised.

It's thirty years since she was launched
And nineteen years since Hastings
And Lady Nelson battles on
And weathers all the bastings!

She's used in films and weddings,
Sails the harbour, scatters ashes,
And now and then has crossed Bass Strait
Where wind and waves bring crashes.

Your purchase of this jingle
Will help keep her neat and trim.
And fill our empty coffers
Right up to the brim!

Thank You!

Margaret Eldridge, July 2018

Role player for the medics

The government urged older Australians to remain in the workforce. (They didn't say how employers would be encouraged to employ us.) However, I managed to work until 82 because, for many years, I was a role player for the Medical Faculty.

Yes, I was paid to have fun! It only stopped because Covid rules did not allow anyone over 65 to enter the Medical Faculty. We were considered the "vulnerable elderly". I was known as Dame Margaret, the doyenne of role players!

I have a certificate on my study wall thanking me for "Outstanding Service".

Medical School End of Year Gathering

I'm a role play patient for the medics,
Or sometimes the patient's wife.
I've had so many sick conditions
I should have lost my life!

I've had meningococcal headaches
UTIs and mental stuff.
I've been asked to be 'quite difficult';
You would think they'd had enough.

My "husband" in emergency
Was not receiving care.
At least that's how I saw it,
His condition was not rare.

"Now can you be obstreperous,
And be a drama queen?
Some tears would make it genuine,
The best we've ever seen".

I've held my head and stomach,
I've cried and carried on;
I've been angry and despondent
I've been shivery and wan.

But whatever ailment I have had,
They've none of them been real;
I'm a hale and hearty patient;
I just pretend it's sick I feel.

The OSCE students get quite nervous,
The stations are a test.
While most of them get passes,
I'm afraid they fail the rest!

A Standardised Patient Finally Accepts the Inevitable

(Or as Michael Beresford would say, 'Dame Margaret is departing' 2020.)

Time to call it a day I think,
But oh! what fun it's been,
Taking on such disparate roles
And sometimes being mean.

The ailments I've experienced
Have gone from bad to worse,
And some have been so very sad
And others just a curse.

I've "suffered" pain and trauma,
You'd have thought that I was dying,
Dementia's taken over
And I've had to give up trying!

I've cried and moaned and panted,
I've heaved great sighs as well.
I've doubled over, bent with pain,
Such stories I can tell.

OSCEs need a lot of work,
Staying strong in role,
Supporting those examiners,
Giving heart and soul.

Simulations, training,
"Communications" too,
Despairing sometimes, truly
At what med. students do not do!

I've worked with many students,
Been horrified by grammar,
Pronunciation, dreadful,
And no idea of bedside manner!

Margaret Eldridge, retiring
standardised patient December 2020

But others have inspired me,
They've shown just what it takes
To produce a well-trained doctor,
Good for all our sakes.

I'd done the job for many years,
Then Michael came along.
Professionally trained I was
And I learned what I did wrong!

I met the other "patients"
And even trained up others,
Michael put his stamp on us
A well-trained band of brothers (and sisters!)

The training videos were fun,
I'm there for all to see,
In perpetuity, so it's sure
You'll go on seeing me!

You may have heard me now and then
Say docs should be super-trained,
And if I've had a hand in this
Everyone has gained!

It's hard to say goodbye right now;
I'll miss the cut and thrust,
But recently, at the receiving end,
Retire I think I must.

Those medics that I've helped to train,
Once green behind the ears;
There must be hundreds, if not more
I've dealt with down the years.

Thank you all for trusting me
To train them up for working
With at least 15 years involvement
I can't be accused of shirking!

Old and New

I have been a client of the South Hobart Tip Shop since it opened and had to put it on record. Along with this, I have enjoyed fossicking in op shops since the early 80s, when I introduced my ESL students to the benefits of recycling.

I also make reference to my struggles with computers, I really only started using one when preparing my Masters. I did a course at TAFE but have always needed assistance. This is where offering a home to students and asylum seekers has really paid off. There has usually been someone in the chalet or the spare room, who could offer assistance and I thank them one and all!

I won't tell you how many things I have "lost" in preparing this book!!!

Photo courtesy of Minh Hien and Farshid

In Praise of Op Shops

Op Shops are a great delight,
I've shopped in them for years.
The price of things at Myer
Had driven me to tears.

Op shops are really popular;
They offer bargains too,
Though someone else has worn the clothes,
Or maybe quite a few!

Sometimes op shop bargains
Are obviously brand new
With labels still attached,
Believe me, this is true.

There's racks and racks of clothing,
Spread for all to see.
Find your size and fashion
And well-dressed you will be.

Find that special outfit,
I did and that's for sure.
I wore it to my 80th,
$15 was the score.

Things may need some alterations,
But that that really does not matter;
Let out a seam or add a tuck,
But don't get any fatter!

Op Shops have variety,
They don't just offer fashion;
You need to keep an open mind
And follow up your passion.

Crockery and cutlery,
Op shops offer plenty;
Novelties and quirky things
Price varies, one to twenty.

Usually there's lots of books
And these are such a treasure,
At prices lower than the shops,
Value beyond measure.

Furniture at op shops
Can prove a great delight.
You'll need to do some polishing
To be exactly right.

Op shops often benefit
Charities and good causes,
So buying things from op shops
Increases their resources.

So give a cheer for op shops,
Where bargains may be found.
Dress for less and look real smart
Take my advice, it's sound.

September 2022

The South Hobart Tip Shop

When I need retail therapy
I head off to the tip.
South Hobart, McRobie's Gully,
It's not a lengthy trip.

The items that they have for sale
Are like Aladdin's Cave,
And fossicking there is such good fun;
The dollars that I save!

I bought a lovely desk you know,
Made of blackwood timber,
And my friend Stan repaired it
In the days when he was limber.

It only cost me twenty bucks
And polished up so well;
It's much admired by different friends,
They're jealous I can tell!

A very favourite armchair
Cost about the same.
I've got it in the kitchen,
Smart seating for this dame!

Another lovely armchair
Is Edwardian in style,
I saw it at the tip shop
But left it for a while.

It didn't sell. Heart ruled head,
I bought it, couldn't help it don't you know.
One day I'll reupholster it
And then compliments will flow.

All sorts of trinkets can be found,
Cutlery and crocks;
Glassware by the boxload
And knitting wool for socks!

There's things there for the garden,
Quite often there are plants;
You needn't spend a fortune.
Go get goodies at a glance!

Matting for my hallway,
Tumblers on my shelf;
You really need to visit
And see it for yourself.

Fabric for the asking,
Stationery of all kinds,
Clothing cheap and stylish
And books, venetian blinds!

Don't say "I can't afford it",
Just visit Hobart tip
And see what bargains you can find,
Be bold and just let rip!

I must have saved a fortune
And I 've had lots of fun,
My bank balance has barely suffered
When all is said and done.

Recycling and upcycling
Are the best ways to go,
Avoiding wasteful landfill.
You'll all agree I know!

September 2022

Computers for the Aged

This grandma knows the feeling,
Computer, friend or foe?
She often has some worries
Re where her emails go.

When in a splint her hand was,
She typed with one hand only,
Responding to her emails
So she would not get lonely.

But problems there were plenty,
The splint bashed on "control"
And shortcuts by the hundred
Appeared and took their toll.

The emails, they all vanished,
They never got to "send"
And grandma retired in fury
For her problems had no end!

"Ask the younger generation
To help you when you're stuck",
But my next generation
Dropped me in the muck.

Dear Edward, can you help me?
I have a problem here.
But Ed wiped my email folder totally
No emails could appear!

"Well, Nanna do not worry,
It's really only a folder.
Put it down to experience,
It's just that you are older"!

Edward left my study.
He didn't seem too worried.
I had to call the expert in.
And that cost lots. Quite torrid!

My Poems

I end this book with three poems.

I do write serious stuff every so often but it takes much more effort than dashing off a jingle.

The first was written when I visited Tam Pui in Laos, the scene of a dreadful tragedy when an American bomber pilot shot a bomb into a large cave where people were hiding from the warfare during the Secret War.

The second poem pays tribute to McAulay Reserve which backs on to my property and gives me unending delight, be it the wattle blossoms, the magnificent eucalyptus or the multitude of bird life.

The last poem *Dream, Shine and Seek to Mend,* was written in response to a sculpture created by Michael Henderson with the same title. It was shown at our church as part of the Luminous festival which is held each year and is always challenging. The underlying theme was reconciliation with indigenous Tasmanians.

Margaret creating jewellery, fund-raising for Motor Neurone Disease Research

Photo courtesy of Minh Hien and Farshid

The War That Never Was

Tears fall where once a missile fell.

No random weapon this.

We stand in the entrance to Tam Pui cave

And adults weep like children,

Sensing the futility, unable to change history.

Oh to be able to talk a while with those who died,

To explain we did not know the dreadful toll;

To be able to rebuild their innocent lives

And understand the deception and duplicity

That led to their deaths and more.

How has the pilot spent his life?

Have remorse and guilt filled his years?

Are the lives of those he killed a weight upon his soul?

Was he a victim of his country's crazed compulsion?

One hundred years! We who weep will be dead and gone

As will more victims of the war that never was,

Before munitions are finally removed,

Before it will be safe to plough again.

Too long! Too late for Laos and her people,

Twice over casualties of the Secret War.

2004

Written after visiting Tam Pui cave, Laos where many Hmong were killed by an American fighter pilot in the Secret War.

McAulay's Reserve

It is mine.

At least it feels that way.

Not well known or prepossessing

It sits in suburbia

But parts recall former times

When grasslands were pristine

And weeds did not infest.

Now two remnant spots remain,

Tended and loved by Bush-care folk,

Recalling times gone by.

Macrocarpa trees,

Not endemic to this place,

Visitors, planted by the old professor

Who used to own this land,

His house still nestles on the fringe.

He knew the value of this corridor.

Blue gums and other eucalypts,

Sentinels along the creek.

Under storey native hops and prickly acacia,

Home for myriad birds which love this space.

Possums abound and build their dreys,

And just occasionally a straying wallaby.

It is ours, to share.

Receiving Welcome: Dream, Shine and Seek to Mend

Why didn't I know?
All those years ago,
New to this Great South Land,
No-one spoke the truth.
No-one told me that all round me
Were those who held on to their aboriginal culture
Over any other influences.
Why didn't I know they were here?
And why didn't I know they were unrecognised,
Had no status, had no vote
It took Harry Penrith, Burnum Burnum,
To help me understand,
He sat at our table, shared our bread,
Explained the hurt, the anger, the grief.
But still, I did not find the Tasmanian remnants,
Those whose hurt and loss I would one day feel.

"What a lovely tan you have" I said to my friend.
His reply surprised me,
"It helps to have aboriginal heritage on both sides".
And then I remembered his mother at a family gathering.
There was a distinctive likeness amongst them all.
I began to recognise what I had overlooked
And then a lovely friendship with Auntie Ida West.
Too short, too brief but her story of Wybalenna
Stayed in my memory.
Finally, a pilgrimage to that place she talked of,
I saw for myself the desolation and neglect.
I heard the hurt and sadness from Auntie Vicky.
She shared her story and tradition.
We collected the dainty maremmer shells with her.
Painted ladies and echidna quills
Created into necklaces so beautiful
They brought tears to my eyes.
How ashamed I am that it has taken years
To begin to understand, and to try to make amends.
Time to Breathe,
Dream, Shine and Seek to Mend.
Time to Receive Welcome.

All good things come to an end

I hope you have had some fun reading through this miscellany.

I really wanted to make people smile and that is what my jingles are about.

Maybe you will be inspired to write some pieces of your own.

Sally jokingly asked me if I would be writing a jingle for my funeral.

My initial reaction was that it would be inappropriate.

Then, I had second thoughts and realised that my friends always expect a jingle on special occasions (and I hope my funeral will be a special occasion!)

So, I've written one for my funeral, but you will have to be there to hear it!!!

Margaret and Sally

Photo courtesy of Minh Hien and Farshid